OCEANSIDE PUBLIC LIBRARY
330 N COAST HWY
OCEANSIDE, CA 92054

P9-DHQ-778

Civic Center
DISCARD

MAKING WAVES

My Journey to
Winning Olympic Gold
and Defeating the
East German Doping Program

Shirley Babashoff
with Chris Epting

Preface by Mark Spitz
Foreword by Donna de Varona

SANTA
MONICA
PRESS

©2016 by Shirley Babashoff and Chris Epting

All rights reserved.

This book may not be reproduced in whole or in part or in any form or format without the written permission of the publisher.

Published by:
Santa Monica Press LLC
P.O. Box 850
Solana Beach, CA 92075
1-800-784-9553

www.santamonicapress.com
books@santamonicapress.com

Printed in the United States

Santa Monica Press books are available at special quantity discounts when purchased in bulk by corporations, organizations, or groups. Please call our Special Sales department at 1-800-784-9553.

This book is intended to provide general information. The publisher, author, distributor, and copyright owner are not engaged in rendering professional advice or services. The publisher, author, distributor, and copyright owner are not liable or responsible to any person or group with respect to any loss, illness, or injury caused or alleged to be caused by the information found in this book.

ISBN-13 978-1-59580-087-9

Library of Congress Cataloging-in-Publication Data

Names: Babashoff, Shirley, 1957- | Epting, Chris, 1961-
Title: Making waves : my journey to winning Olympic Gold and defeating the East German Doping Program / by Shirley Babashoff with Chris Epting ; foreword by Donna de Varona.
Description: Solana Beach, CA : Santa Monica Press LLC, [2016] | Includes bibliographical references and index.
Identifiers: LCCN 2016007635 (print) † LCCN 2016019549 (ebook) | ISBN 9781595800879 (Hardcover) | ISBN 9781595808028 (PDF ebook) | ISBN 9781595808035 (Kindle) | ISBN 9781595808042 (Epub)
Subjects: LCSH: Babashoff, Shirley, 1957- | Women swimmers--United States--Biography. | Olympics--History--20th century. | Doping in sports--History--Germany (East)
Classification: LCC GV838.B34 A3 2016 (print) | LCC GV838.B34 (ebook) | DDC
797.2/1092 [B] --dc23
LC record available at https://lccn.loc.gov/2016007635

Cover and interior design and production by Future Studio

MIX
Paper fr
responsible
FSC   FSC® CO
www.fsc.org

31232009913031

Dedication

**This book is dedicated to my teammates
from the 1976 Olympic Games:**

Melissa Belote, Wendy Boglioli , Brenda Borgh,
Lelei Fonoimoana, Maryanne Graham, Jeanne Haney,
Janis Hape, Kathy Heddy, Jennifer Hooker, Linda Jezek,
Nicole Kramer, Renee Laravie, Renee Magee, Marcia Morey,
Kim Peyton, Lauri Siering, Miriam Smith, Jill Sterkel,
Karen Thornton, Tauna Vandeweghe, Wendy Weinberg,
Donna Lee Wennerstrom, and Camille Wright.

Contents

7 PREFACE by Mark Spitz

9 FOREWORD by Donna de Varona

13 INTRODUCTION

19 Chapter 1: **Growing Up**

29 Chapter 2: **And So It Begins . . .**

43 Chapter 3: **My First Adventure**

55 Chapter 4: **A New Coach**

61 Chapter 5: **Munich**

77 Chapter 6: **Feeling Like a Celebrity**

85 Chapter 7: **What Happened to the East Germans?**

95 Chapter 8: **Skinsuits and a Mysterious Vaccine**

101 Chapter 9: **Swimming with the College Boys**

111 Chapter 10: **My Personal Best**

123 Chapter 11: **Training for '76**

133 Chapter 12: **The Montreal Games**

143 Chapter 13: **Forming a Strategy**

153 Chapter 14: **The Final Race**

169 Chapter 15: **A National Disgrace**

183   Chapter 16: **Marriage**

191   Chapter 17: **The Charade Continues**

199   Chapter 18: **New Beginnings**

211   Chapter 19: **The Cheaters**

219   Chapter 20: **The Olympic Order**

229   Chapter 21: **The Truth Comes Out**

239   Chapter 22: **My Future Is Now**

245   SHIRLEY BABASHOFF'S INDIVIDUAL
WORLD AND AMERICAN RECORDS

247   AN OPEN LETTER TO THOMAS BACH, PRESIDENT OF
THE INTERNATIONAL OLYMPIC COMMITTEE

249   WHAT THE 1976 OLYMPIC RECORDS WOULD LOOK LIKE
IF THEY WERE REVISED

255   NOTES FROM COACHES JIM MONTRELLA AND
MARK SCHUBERT

261   ABOUT THE AUTHORS

263   ACKNOWLEDGMENTS

265   INDEX

272   PHOTO CREDITS

Preface

by Mark Spitz

Shirley, you gave all that you had to give. You saw it in your mind. You never turned away or quit. You sought, and you found. It was that power of your dreams, holding on to hope, that took you much higher.

Your destiny was not a matter of chance, but a matter of the choices you made. It wasn't something that you waited around for, but rather achieved. You saw things that never were and said, "Why not?" You became a champion, you became a leader, you became you—a true Olympian. You lived for your tomorrows like only you could, with dignity.

So, we celebrate you, Shirley Babashoff, and your Olympic performances. The tradition goes on, a tradition that is more than two thousand years old. The call has been the same throughout history: *Citius, Altius, Fortius.* "Faster, Higher, Stronger." It is the call that you took, and you inspired us with your talent, pride, dedication, and courage.

You stood on the victory podium with the finest in the world. You reached for that never ending pursuit of excellence, and that is the way it should be. What you did has become the standard for generations not yet born. You achieved and excelled, and history has recorded it as the measure of your greatness.

We celebrate in tribute to you, Shirley, what you so richly earned. It is your time and turn to be recognized. Let this book renew your incredible success.

Your honored teammate and friend,
MARK SPITZ
1972 Olympian

Foreword
by Donna de Varona

Shirley Babashoff was a true victim of a time in sports when those responsible for competitive swimming were either naive or chose to turn a blind eye to the entourage of cheats invading the pool decks and playing fields of international sport.

Shirley competed during the darkest years of sports—a time when the Eastern Bloc countries, especially East Germany, created an elaborate sports system that force-fed performance-enhancing drugs to its elite athletes.

The World Anti-Doping Agency and the U.S. Anti-Doping Agency weren't established until after the Sydney Olympics in 2000. Sadly, the absence of extensive testing, both in and out of competition, during Shirley's active years and beyond left the sporting world vulnerable to those determined to cheat.

In 1973, I covered the first-ever FINA World Swimming Championships in Belgrade, Yugoslavia, for ABC. Contrary to how countries traditionally emerge as sports rivals, the East German women's team came out of nowhere to dominate the competition. What we witnessed was the emergence of a sinister sports machine that threatened to undermine all that is sacred in sports. The East German women were used as experimental guinea pigs in an effort to showcase a communist system using sports for political gain.

Caught up in this collision course of fanatical Cold War gamesmanship were the innocents. Shirley was one of them. Before the 1976 Montreal Olympics, she had become America's golden girl. The media burdened her with the expectation of equaling Mark Spitz's seven-gold-medal haul during the 1972 Munich Games. This was unfair and set Shirley and her teammates up for failure, especially given the East Germans' steroid-infused performance.

As someone who covered those Games for ABC, I could only hint at what was going on behind the scenes. With no extensive drug testing, I could not accuse the East Germans outright of cheating. It was painful to witness the international press eager to beat up on our women's team—especially Shirley, because she did not win any individual gold medals. It was frustrating to watch what little support both the U.S. swimming and USOC executives provided to our brave athletes when they finally began to point fingers at the East German team as the Montreal swimming events drew to a close.

The cost of these leaders' inaction cannot be measured on any level; their failure to protect the sport created generations of cheats both outside and inside the U.S. It also allowed the East German government to continue to abuse its own athletes, many of whom suffered lifetimes of depression, guilt, and health problems. Even after it was proven that the East Germans used performance-enhancing drugs, neither FINA (the international governing body for swimming) nor the IOC provided any sort of remedy for those whose Olympic medals were stolen from them.

Until recently, Shirley spent a lifetime disconnected from a sport and community she once trusted and loved. She was always reluctant to bask in the spotlight, preferring to let her performances speak for her. I can only imagine how differently her life would have unfolded if she had competed on a level playing field.

I'm grateful Shirley is finally telling her story. It is a cautionary tale, and one every athlete, coach, administrator, and parent should read.

Introduction

During a relay, all that has to be touching the side of the pool is the swimmer's fingernail. And all that has to be touching the starting block is their toenail.

I keep thinking that.

Just her fingernail, and just my toenail. Those are the rules in the relay. As I'm standing on the block, watching Jill Sterkel swim toward me, that's what I'm thinking about, because she has a slight lead right now. This tough and tenacious fifteen-year-old actually has a lead. And if I'm going to keep that lead, I'm literally going to need the best relay exchange of my life.

This is probably the loudest crowd I've ever heard. It's almost surreal to be standing on this platform.

Is this really happening?

This is the last race of the Olympics and our last chance to win gold. It wasn't supposed to be like this. This is not what everybody expected. We were not supposed to be fighting for our dignity. But we are.

I'm getting ready. Come on, Jill. Hold that lead. Remember what we all talked about in our dorm room last night. What you're doing right now is unbelievable. You've actually taken the lead, and that's why the crowd is going so crazy. Nobody thought we would be in this position right now. After this insane last week or so, it's been all about the East Germans—how wonderful and talented they are, and what a disappointment we American girls are.

Most of the girls on the team were intimidated coming into these Olympics. But now they're just demoralized. It's such a weird thing to walk into the locker room and find what you think are guys in there. And then it turns out that it's actually a female swimming team, one that is now beating you day in and day out, that comes from a country one fraction the size of yours, and that, all of a sudden, is producing some of the strongest swimmers in history over the course of just a couple of years.

But hey, why should any of that seem suspicious? Why should anybody take notice except me, a Southern California girl with a penchant for speaking her mind?

We can't help it if we're not cheating. We can't help it if all we do is play by the rules. I've been swimming twenty miles a day for the past four years. How much more was I supposed to swim? I've been setting what would have been world records, were it not for these grotesque mutations otherwise known as the female East German swimming team.

But right now, none of that matters. Nobody wants to hear that right now. All that matters is the lead that Jill has. Because that little lead may help produce one of the biggest upsets in Olympics history.

But we're not there yet. I still have to close this thing out.

Focus has never been much of an issue for me in my swimming career. I know how to focus and I know how to win. Sometimes I feel like a machine. But right now, it's a bit of a challenge to stay completely focused in the moment. If we win, will the press stop calling me names? Will it be the end of "Surly Shirley"?

If we win, will the coaches and officials and media finally open their damned eyes and start looking into this team of so-called women that look and sound like men?

Okay, Jill is getting closer. One thing that used to frustrate me was watching how swimmers would wait to wind up for the take-off until their teammates actually touched the edge of the pool. That's a lot of time wasted. If you start your wind-up early and then dive in the air, timing the other swimmers touch perfectly, you can pick up a good deal of time.

Of course, a good deal of time is a relative term. We're talking about a sport in which a tenth of a second and a hundredth of a second actually matter. But executed perfectly, there was definitely a chunk of time to be made on the start.

I'm not going to wait for her to touch before winding up. I've got to watch her closely, just like we all talked about last night, just like we play-acted in our dorm room, as we were living out the race over and over and over in preparation for this moment. Was that really just last night? It seems so long ago. I never thought those positive thinking courses they wanted us all to take would ever come in handy, but last night, they sort of did. Lying there on the bunk bed, zoning out and imagining that we were all swimming the race at the same time, it really was sort of interesting. I think it helped. And at this point, what did we have to lose?

We were using anything we could get. Even those matching rainbow suspenders we all bought. Sure, maybe it was just a gimmick, but for us, it was fun and it made us look and feel like more of a team. Walking out on that deck, everybody seemed to notice it too. So maybe it was a good idea after all.

When you're going up against a demon team like this, never know what's going to work. You have to try everything.

Okay, I'm focused. The crowd is beginning to fade away, and the tunnel in my mind is starting to tighten and narrow. The moment is at hand.

Jill, you are amazing. I almost can't believe you've taken the lead like this. Of the many teams I've swam with over the years, all over the world in hundreds of competitions, I don't think I've ever been prouder than I am of the three girls I walked out on the deck with today.

I'm the last in this relay. If I can hold this lead, then we will achieve what many considered to be impossible.

Here she comes. Okay, Shirley. Don't leave early, be careful, and don't be too anxious.

Winding up, I see Jill's final stroke as she's about to touch the wall, and I explode into the air. I've never left with such force in my life. Every ounce of my body, every muscle in my system is dialed into this moment. It's never felt better.

But in the back of my head, something is wrong. The second I hit the water, I think to myself, I left too early. In my zeal to achieve the perfect start, I cheated the clock just a bit.

Her fingernail.

My toenail.

My entire world now comes down to whether or not I waited long enough for her fingernail to touch that wall before taking off.

But as I hit the water, I also think to myself, it doesn't matter. They're not going to stop the race. If I did in fact leave early, then once I finish the race and look up, I will see the little red dot by my name on the scoreboard. That will mean I've been flagged for an early start.

But that's not important right now. All that's important right now is that I just put my head down and go. Just go, go, go, go, go, go. Everything else will sort itself out in the end.

Right now, I'm in the water and I need to hold this lead. Almost instantly, upon impact, the roar of the crowd is back in my head.

Only now, it's louder. My start has caused the crowd to erupt even further, and I can hear them with each breath— thousands of people screaming like maniacs for me to hold that lead. Thousands of people who seem to know that there's been something very wrong at these Olympics. Thousands of people who want me to finish this thing the right way.

It's so weird where life takes you. I was a skinny little girl that no swim team ever wanted. My mother would actually use me as a bargaining chip when teams wanted my brothers instead. You have to take Shirley, too, she would tell them. And so, begrudgingly, they did.

I wonder if any of those coaches remember me?

Are they watching me on television right now?

Are they here, cheering for me?

You will never have another moment like this, I keep thinking to myself. This is a sprint, one length down and one length back. This is what I've worked for. I can do this. God, I can do this. I have to do this.

Swim, Shirley, swim.

Listen to that crowd and let them feel you.

You know how to do this. You can do this.

You're going to beat these cheaters.

You have to.

CHAPTER ONE

Growing Up

I can still smell that old army tent in the backyard. My father, who had taught swimming while in the army in Hawaii, had rigged one of his old tents into a makeshift swimming pool behind our modest house in the Los Angeles suburb of Norwalk. It was musty and oily and really sort of rank. Its odor was distinctive, especially when the tent was filled with water. It could hardly be called a swimming pool. It was just a place where my two brothers and I splashed around.

Our house in Norwalk was located in a fairly typical blue-collar neighborhood for the 1950s—a three-bedroom, one-bathroom, single-story suburban dwelling. Any person coming up the walk to the front door would see the dining room table with open bibles and a Russian samovar. The people living here must have been moral and upstanding, right? Wrong. At least, not the parents.

My brothers and I rode a bus to school, which wasn't that far from the house, but there was a busy street and two cow pastures to pass by. The house was in a relatively rural area (today, like a lot of Southern California communities, the area around the neighborhood has been heavily developed).

I always hung around my two brothers—Jack, one and a half years older than me, and Bill, two years younger. I always felt like Bill was a burden, but I'm sure Jack thought the same of me. We would mostly explore the neighborhood, riding bikes, skateboarding, digging in the dirt, and, of course, fighting. But our parents fought a lot, too, and we were terrified that they would get a divorce. At night, Jack would say, "If they get a divorce, we're all going to have to go live in a foster home and those places are next to hell." So we would huddle together, scared, and ride out the storm of their arguments.

Given how gray and shapeless our family life was, I suppose that little pool in the backyard was actually pretty important. It was a chance for us to have a little fun at home, a respite from the usual dreariness and sometimes outright misery that defined my earliest years.

My parents, Jack and Vera Babashoff, were of Russian heritage, and they were true to the stereotype. They were cold and stoic and never really communicated with me or my brothers. It was not a loving, warm, and nurturing environment. On the contrary, it was cold, distant, and, at times, quite destructive.

They were part of the Russian Molokan Church, a strict and unforgiving faith that was taken very seriously in our household. If my brothers or I ever spoke one negative word toward each other, punishments were swift and sometimes cruel. I'm talking about basic disagreements between siblings. None of it was allowed. Understanding the rules early in life, the three of us tiptoed through our childhood, trying not to upset our parents.

My mother was the daughter of a strict preacher. She never really had anything nice to say about the man, only about how he really had nothing to do with her. She grew up on farms in Northern California and in Oregon. I remember her telling us that she had to walk miles in the snow just to catch the school bus. I know that's like a joke today, but when she said it, she wasn't being funny. It was real. After she finished high school, she and my dad were married.

When my mom was pregnant with my younger brother, the doctors found a growth in her neck. They removed it, but her health was never the same again. After that, she became addicted to pain pills and whatever else she could get the doctors to give her. From that point on, it was as if she lived in a big, puffy cloud. She was always kind of out of it, and pill bottles were always scattered all over the place. I think it was partly her addiction that prevented her from really being much of a parent.

My father was one of seven boys who were all born in the 1920s. He grew up in Los Angeles and started working as a machinist at Bethlehem Steel when he was just sixteen years old. He never finished high school, but always lied on his résumé about his education and age. In fact, he rarely told the truth, it seems.

My parents spoke Russian when they were hiding things from us. My brothers and I were never taught the language, so we never had any idea what they were talking about. I remember once in the sixth grade, all of the kids were discussing their heritage. Most of the kids in my class had hybrid origins—Swedish-German or French-English or Irish-Italian. I was all Russian, and that was horrible. Once, all the kids in my class called me a "commie."

At home, being Russian was hugely important to my mom. We went to a church that only allowed Russians on Sundays. On Mondays, we went to a Boys and Girls Club for Russians only. At home, we were forbidden to eat anything that was not kosher. We would pray before dinner in Russian. On family holidays, we spent time with all of our extended Russian family members.

An aunt and uncle of mine had some money, and their home had a beautiful swimming pool that looked like something out of an Elvis Presley movie in Palm Springs. The pool was surrounded by beautiful palm trees, and her home was a classic mid-century modern design. I just loved going there. My family also frequently took short and affordable trips either to local beaches or nearby lakes.

My brothers and I loved the water. Even though my dad had been a swimming teacher, he was not the one pushing us to be swimmers. That was my mother, who had such an extreme fear of the water that she wanted to make sure none of us followed in her footsteps. She was always panicked that something would happen to us in the water, which was why she enrolled us in swimming classes early on.

I was eight years old when I started taking swimming lessons at Cerritos College, which wasn't too far from our house. While I loved playing around in the water, I wasn't too crazy about the lessons. To get us used to staying underwater, they would make us hold on to what was called a "shepherd's crook," which was basically a long pole with a hook on the end of it. While kids held onto the hook, the instructor pushed the pole to the bottom of the pool and held them down there. I absolutely hated it. Whenever I had to do it, it made my ears really uncomfortable, so I would shimmy up the pole as far as I could to get closer to the surface. This always made the instructors really mad.

I also wasn't comfortable with the fact that, because I was just a beginning swimmer, I was placed in a group with five-year-olds. That was so embarrassing for me. They were practically toddlers. But it was what my mother wanted me to do, so I didn't dare speak up. That was the rule. I would just cry.

Since I hated taking swimming lessons there, we switched to the Norwalk High School pool, where the classes were regulated by the Red Cross. In fact, my very first race happened at the end of that summer, when I swam against another girl in a single twenty-five-yard length. I hadn't even learned side breathing yet, so as we were racing, whenever it was time for me to breathe, I would stop, dog paddle for a moment, take a breath, watch her pass me, and then keep swimming to try and catch up. As ridiculous as that sounds, I actually won the race. But before I even had a moment to enjoy and savor my accomplishment, I was shocked to see the little girl's father rush over to the edge of the pool, grab her out of the water by her arm, and begin yelling at her for losing to me. "How can you be slow?" he yelled. "She's not a swimmer. *You're* a swimmer! Start acting like it!"

Wow, I thought to myself, is that going to happen to me if I ever lose a race?

My older brother, Jack, was a really strong swimmer. When my mom decided to sign us up for a club team, the coach wanted Jack, not me. But my mother always made me part of the package and explained to those in charge that if they didn't take me, then they couldn't have Jack. It was the first of many times that this would happen in my life. Nobody ever wanted me, but they wanted Jack so badly that I got tossed in as the add-on. It was crushing for me was to have to stand there and listen to my mother explain to the coach that, no matter how much they didn't want me, they still had to take me.

When I was about nine years old, we joined a team called the Buena Park Splashers. Again, they desperately wanted my brother, but in order to have him on board, they also had to take me. I could see how mad it made the coaches to have my mother forcing me on them, but they would always bite the bullet and allow me to swim on the team.

I was a fairly good academic student around this time and actually got to skip the fourth grade, which meant that every day I would be walking to Norwalk Brethren, a private school nearby. It was maybe a half-mile away or so, which wasn't too far, but we had neighbors who always worried about me. My parents showed no concern, but more than one person living on our street would always tell me when they saw me, "Shirley, you have to be careful when you walk by yourself. You can't ever talk to strangers. You never know what might happen if you do. You really need to be careful."

I always listened to them. I understood their concerns. To my neighbors, the streets were potentially dangerous and unkind. But had they known what was happening in my own home, they probably would've called the police. At least, I hope they would have.

I don't know when it started. I didn't know what it was. But I knew I didn't like it.

I'm not completely sure when I first became aware of the fact that my father was molesting me. Of course, by the time I was in the third and fourth grade, I knew exactly what was happening. He would creep into my room late at night and wake me up. Then, quickly and quietly, he would remove my underwear.

I told him to stop, but he said things like "This is what daddies do." Each time I told him no, he said, "It's what daughters and daddies do." I told him I would tell Mom, and he said she would call me a liar.

I don't know how my mom didn't hear me cry. When I was five years old, I said to her, "Daddy comes into my room at night and touches me." My father was right—she called me a liar and told me to never say that again. Then she got the bible out and made me read the fifth commandment: Obey your mother and father.

Later on in life, she would say to me, "I don't know what happened. You were always daddy's little girl until you turned about five years old. Then you didn't want anything to do with him." Well of course not. That's when I had realized what he was doing to me.

That's the disgusting monster that my father was. I was so afraid at night. I kept thinking that if anyone found out, I might have to go to a foster home, just like my brother had warned. So I went on, never knowing why it was happening to me.

This is the hardest thing to talk about. But I couldn't write this book without including it, knowing how many women and children he has hurt. To portray him as something else would be a lie.

It went on for years. I asked my mom to put a lock on my door, but she accused me of trying to hide something. Yes, I *was* trying to hide something. She was right. I was trying to hide myself.

It was so strange, because I would rarely see my father due to his work hours. He worked all the time. Not just at his job at the plant, but at a drive-in movie theater, too. Yet this was how he chose to spend our time together. He'd wait until the house was dark and quiet. When it would happen, I remember not allowing my mind to even try to process what was taking place. I would lose myself in some other world and imagine myself in some far-off, tranquil pool, by myself—away from the monster that was violating me. I had no other escape.

My own father.

Looking back on it today and analyzing my earliest years, I am fairly sure these horrors began taking place shortly after I was born. When I think about my parents' behavior, it speaks to a very dark and haunting pattern in my life.

I remember when I was in the first grade, there was a teacher who was concerned about me. Even though these were the days when society was far more oblivious about things like child molestation, this teacher of mine must have sensed that something was wrong with me. I'm sure there are certain telltale signs that a smart teacher can pick up on and begin to get suspicious about.

She called my mother down to the school to have a little discussion about me and what might be happening at home. As I sat there, nervous and biting my nails (which was becoming a bad habit for me), my mother denied anything of the sort. "Mrs. Babashoff," my teacher began, gently and diplomatically, "is everything okay at home? Shirley gets withdrawn at times, and distant. She's a very bright young girl. We're here to help if we can."

"There is nothing wrong in our home," my mother insisted adamantly. "She's just shy. And I don't appreciate any suggestion that something is wrong in our household. We work very hard at raising our family, my husband and me."

On the way home, my mother just glared at me in the car, as if I'd had anything to do with setting up the meeting.

I remember once in the fifth grade, I was in the school bathroom by myself when a friend came in. I decided to confide in her about what was happening at home, to see if this was something other people knew about. Stammering once or twice, I finally choked out the words: "My dad takes my underwear off. He tells me that's what all dads do. And then he touches me. And other things. He says all dads do this. Does your dad do that?"

Instantly, I was sorry that I had said anything at all. Understandably, my friend became very agitated and started yelling at me, "You can't say that, shut up, that can't be true, I don't believe you!"

I regretted telling her, but I was so confused. I just needed to reach out to someone, anyone, yet I was too scared to speak to adults about it. God only knows what my mother would have done to me, had she known I even brought it up to my friend in the bathroom.

Somehow or another, I managed to get up and go to school each day and also keep swimming in a variety of clubs during those early years. As a child, I guess you just get sort of numb. The whole situation seemed so futile that I decided there really was no way out and the best course of action was simply to focus on things I could control. Again, this was long before the days when people looked for things like this or when kids had outlets they could go to and cry for help.

Later on in life, when *Sports Illustrated* did a feature about me around the time of the 1976 Summer Olympics, the writer came and stayed with us for a couple of days and wrote the following:

> *They are closer and stronger than the Waltons. They go to church on Sunday and visit their grandparents regularly. They say grace at meals and eschew spirits. The children do as they are told and use no bad language. The parents are self-sacrificing and, as is said nowadays, supportive. Everybody helps out and there are few complaints. Vera and Jack Babashoff are frugal, honest, industrious, and the source of the strength that helps set Shirley apart from her peers.*

There was more, about how hardworking and decent and wonderful my parents were. It was just another example of how different the world was at that point. A little research on the writer's part might have revealed many compelling things.

When I was thirteen years old, I'd had enough. When he came into my room, I decided to just keep kicking him until he left me alone. He never came into my room again. Later, my mom told me, he became a predator to my younger sister. She also told me that she had threatened him with divorce if he ever did it again. But she never followed up on it. Talk is cheap.

CHAPTER TWO

And So It Begins . . .

When I was about eight years old, my mother started signing me up for private swimming lessons. It was all the way out in the San Fernando Valley, and the lessons were given by an old woman whom I would say was about eighty-five. She had a pool in her yard and, for tax purposes, she was not allowed to accept money for giving lessons. I remember that there was just this big old jar on a table that was full of cash, where people would put their "donations" for the lessons.

The old woman was very focused on making me what she called a "pretty" swimmer; that is to say, she wanted me to have beautiful strokes and something called a "six-beat kick" which meant that you would kick your legs six times per stroke. But I was far from a pretty swimmer. In my head, swimming was all about speed. Whatever it took to swim faster, that's what I was interested in. I had a two-beat kick, which worked better for me. It helped me keep the pace that I wanted, and I was comfortable with it. But it was not very pretty to look at.

My lessons with the old woman didn't last long. I bounced around from place to place, taking private classes at other pools in the area, including the local high school and at a diving school with a teacher named John Riley. Mr. Riley also wanted me to abide by the six-beat kick, but I was having none of it.

Early in my life—at least, when it came to swimming—I became stubborn and didn't do what everybody else wanted me to do. Little did I know what effect this personality trait would have later on.

The chlorine used to kill my eyes, so I started wearing goggles, which were new in the 1960s. Mr. Riley didn't like that and he let me know it, but I didn't care. If I was going to be spending that much time in the water, then I was going to wear goggles.

When I was a kid, it seemed like whenever I started swimming someplace new, there was always some other girl that everyone would say was the best. "She's the one to beat!" "Nobody's going to beat her!" In my head, those were always the ones I set out to beat. I think my brain was wired at an early age to always be thinking about winning.

At one of our swim clubs, located in Bellflower, the one to beat was Sherry Duke. She was the golden child of the pool. Her father was also a local cop and my mother, in her ignorance, never wanted me to beat her for fear of getting a ticket. That was how my parents thought. Looking back, it's almost amazing how clueless they were about life. But her concerns didn't slow me down at all, and eventually, I beat Sherry. When I was eleven years old, I joined a team in El Monte. There, the girl to beat was Cozette Wheeler. She was untouchable, all of the adults said. She was the one that intimidated all of the other kids. Soon after getting there, I beat Cozette.

But that's not what I remember most about swimming in El Monte. What I remember most were two other girls, Jill Sterkel and Sandy Neilson, who were also on the team. Little did I know what the future held for all of us—especially for me and Jill. Thinking back, the coach at that club, Don LaMont, must have been really good to develop swimmers of that caliber—including me and my brothers, Jack and Bill.

With the three of us swimming, my family's weekends were filled with swim meets. In California, where the sun shines almost all year long, we could find a meet practically anywhere. We went to meets in San Diego, Redlands, Los Angeles, Apple Valley, Lakewood, Buena Park, and many other cities.

I loved going to those swim meets. There were hundreds of kids at them. I saw my friends from my own team and made new friends from other teams. I got to see my competition from a wider group of girls—not just from my own club, but from other clubs that were the ones to beat.

Sometimes the meets were far away and we would have to wake up early in the morning to travel there. Other families would stay at a hotel or motel for the weekend, but we would always come home after our meets; we couldn't afford to pay for an overnight stay. Gas was much cheaper then, so after driving home at the end of the day, we would get up early the next day and just drive back to the meet again. My mom always packed food for us, because we needed to eat constantly and we couldn't afford to buy our meals at the meet. She packed hamburgers, bananas, oranges—foods to fill us up.

Our meets started at 9:00 AM, with warm-ups at 8:00 AM. At the warm-ups, you could get a feel for the pool—the walls, the lane markings on the bottom of the pool, and the backstroke flags, which hung above the water at the end of the pool so backstrokers would know the wall was coming. You could count how many strokes until you hit the wall so you wouldn't conk your head.

At those meets, I swam three or four events each day. When I was nine and ten years old, I really liked the breaststroke and freestyle. I never really fell in love with the butterfly, and to be honest, I don't think I really got the hang of it until I was seventeen or eighteen. I knew all the other strokes, though, and that made me a pretty good individual medley swimmer.

There was such a communal feel at those meets. Part of it had to do with the snacks we ate: Jell-O powder right out of the package, pixie sticks, rainbow pops. Sugar everywhere. That's part of what held us together. Then there were the things we did to kill time between the races. I remember everyone playing with Clackers, those hard plastic balls you'd clack together on a string that were eventually taken off the market because they would shatter. It didn't matter, though. We still had plenty of yo-yos, Frisbees, another popular toys to help wile away the time. But the thing I liked best was playing cards. Poker, Twenty-One, War, Go Fish—it was my favorite way to pass the time at the meets.

When I was eleven, my mom became very interested in a woman named Loretta Reed. The Reeds had some money and lived in Rancho Palos Verdes. Mrs. Reed would sit on the pool deck in El Monte, watching her daughter (and my friend) Pam swim alongside me. My mother was quite transfixed with her, impressed with her lifestyle and fancy car. I would always see them talking on the deck of the pool while we swam. I'd never seen my mother so interested in another person. She would sit there, looking at Mrs. Reed's stopwatch, and soon she had a stopwatch of her own that she would use to time my laps.

One day, as we were driving home from one of our club practices, my mother asked me how I did that day and what my times were. I told her I thought I had done well. All of the sudden, she began beating me with her fist. I couldn't figure out what I had done wrong. I pushed myself against the passenger door of our Plymouth station wagon, trying to get out of her reach. But there wasn't enough room for me to get away from her. She was angry that I had not swum better times. It was crazy. These were practices, not races. But she didn't care.

Day after day, the same thing would happen. "How do you think you did today?" she'd ask. "Fine," I'd say. And the beating would start.

One day, as my mother was hitting me in the front seat, Jack, sitting with Bill in the back seat, asked, "Why do you only care about her?" Driving wildly down the freeway and steering with her left hand, she reached back and started hitting him with her right fist. "Is this what you want?" she asked. He never posed the question again.

This began a new pattern of abuse in my life. No matter how I answered my mother's question about my performance, she would start hitting me. This went on for months. My mother would beat me in the car after practice, and then my father would molest me at night.

One day, we actually went to the Reeds' house in Palos Verdes. It was beautiful. While our mothers were having coffee inside, Pam and I sat outside together.

"Does your mom hit you?" she asked me.

"Yeah," I said. "How did you know?"

"Well, my mom beats me, too," she said. "I think she told your mom that it was a good way to make you swim faster."

Thanks a lot, I thought.

I really did enjoy swimming back then, because the pool had become my sanctuary. No matter what took place in the car after swim practice or in my bedroom at night, when I was in the water, I was safe. It was a haven where I could have fun and make friends and get stronger. That was one thing about me—I enjoyed becoming a better swimmer, and I was very competitive. It was all I had in my young life. Besides playing the flute in school, it was really the only other activity that I took part in. So I made the most of it.

The coaches may not have wanted me in the beginning and my parents may have been abusing me, but while I was in the water, I was safe and free to become what I wanted to be: a strong swimmer. That was my plan. But plans change, of course, and for my family, things were about to be altered in a very serious way.

We moved around from pool to pool and I swam on lots of teams. I also began competing and had great success early on.

When I was thirteen, I started swimming on a team at Golden West College in Huntington Beach, California. It was called Phillips 66, and it was sponsored by the Texas energy company of the same name.

This team was significant for me on two levels. First, it got me out of El Monte and away from Loretta Reed, which meant my mom's beatings would stop soon after our·arrival in Huntington Beach. Second, and more importantly, this was where I would meet one of the two most influential coaches I'd ever have.

His name was Ralph Darr but he went by "Flip," and he was one of the most amazing men I have ever met. First of all, he just seemed really cool. He drove a Jaguar and smoked a pipe and there was something very low-key, yet nurturing, about him.

Flip was also an incredibly innovative and successful coach. He eventually coached swimmers that would go on to earn sixteen world records, eight gold medals, nine World Championship medals, the three Pan American Games medals, and thirty-one U.S. national swimming titles. He placed swimmers on the U.S. team in the 1968, '72, '76, and '84 Olympics, and he would go on to serve as the U.S. coach of the 1975 World Championship women's team, the 1991 World Championship open water team, and many others. Flip was also known as one of the first coaches to bring hand paddles into mainstream swimming during practices, which was revolutionary. He also utilized surgical tubes for resistance training—another breakthrough.

But beyond all of that, he was just a really solid guy who took his swimming very seriously and looked after me—at least it seemed that way to me, anyway. He was decent and kind and thoughtful, which I think may have helped save me back then and may have even given me the strength to change my situation.

When I got to Huntington Beach, Susie Whitaker was the girl to beat. And not long after joining the club, I did beat her. But it cost me. She had a big makeup party and I was the only girl not invited simply because I had bested her in the pool. It didn't really bother me, though; I wasn't used to being one of the gang and usually kept to myself anyway. And I didn't care about makeup, or about being popular. I was just there to beat them all.

These victories of mine over the "best" kids gave me kind of an inner strength. Even to this day, I tell young people: "Don't ever give up hope. Wherever you go in life, there's always going to be somebody who's identified as the best. And if you set your sights on it, there's no reason you can't be the one who, one day, everybody will look at as the best."

Again, a lot of this came from an inner sense of competition that I think I was born with. I was also very focused because I blocked out other things happening in my life. That combination really helped me develop into someone who was not only unintimidated by the so-called best on the block, but who also relished the challenge of trying to beat them.

At thirteen years old, I took my first plane trip to Cincinnati for the 1970 Short Course Nationals, which I had qualified for. Getting to the Nationals required hitting a certain time standard in each event. Basically, you had to swim at a sanctioned event and turn in a faster time than the standard in order to be invited to the Nationals. Then, once you were there, you would get seeded based on your times.

The Nationals are held twice each year. They're what you're really training for. Flip was excited the day he told me at practice that I was going.

"Good news, Shirley," he said, his ever-present pipe in hand. "You've qualified. This is a big first step for you. Don't be nervous. Just go have fun. This is how you learn to compete, so don't put any real pressure on yourself."

For our trip, one of the girls' moms, Mrs. Hanson, made matching outfits for all the girls on the swim team: white polyester tops with sweetheart necklines and red skirts.

It felt so great to be on my own for the first time. I didn't do that well in the one race I swam, but it was okay; as Flip had said, I was learning how to compete. I was having a blast, too. It was exciting to fly on a plane and compete at a big event like the Nationals.

I think my first real brush with the media took place when I got back from Cincinnati. Once I was back in junior high, a boy who wrote for the school paper came over to me in the cafeteria. "Do you think I could interview you for an article that I want to write?" he asked. "Sure," I replied. "Why not?" So we met after school, and he conducted his interview.

"Did you have fun in Cincinnati?" he asked.

"Yes," I answered.

"Is it true that this was your first plane ride?"

"Yes."

"Is it tough to swim in those races?"

"Yes."

"Are you going to continue as a swimmer?"

"Yes."

"Was it fun coming back to school?"

"No."

A few days later, the school paper came out. When I got

home that afternoon, my mom was waiting with a copy in her hand. She was not happy. "You really gave these answers to him?" she asked, pointing at the paper in disgust. "This is your idea of how to give an interview?"

"Yes," I answered, without any kind of irony.

My mother explained that, whenever somebody asked me questions, I was not to give yes or no answers. "You have to make a conversation," she said. "You can't just say yes or no. If you want people to learn about you, then you have to give better answers."

I understood what she was saying. It made sense. But what my mother didn't know was that, in the process of teaching me how to do an interview, she probably opened up a bit of a Pandora's box. When the microphones were in front of me in the years to come, I think a lot of people wished that I would just shut up. For now, I would take my mom's advice and try to give more developed answers whenever I was interviewed. However, this process also spawned my lack of trust with the media early on, when I was interviewed by our local newspaper soon after my middle school interview.

As my mother had ordered, I gave what I thought were thoughtful and conversational answers to the questions my interviewer asked me about swimming. But once the paper came out, I saw sections in print that I knew I hadn't spoken. I didn't even know the meaning of some of the words being attributed to me, so how could I have said them in the first place? Such was the beginning of my love-hate relationship with the press.

Back home, it was still a house of horrors. I didn't want anything to happen to my baby sister, but didn't know what to do to protect her, either. I couldn't go to my mother. I don't think my two brothers knew what was going on. I had not told them, and I doubt they had picked up on anything. What was I going to do?

As it turned out, I didn't have to do anything.

One night, there was a knock at our front door. It was in the evening, around eight o'clock or so. My father was at work; the rest of the family was home.

As my mother opened the door, I saw a group of men standing in our doorway, maybe six or seven deep. They all looked very angry and upset.

"Do you know why we're here?" one of them asked my mother.

"Do you know what's going on?" asked another.

My mother just stared back at them, not saying a word.

As I looked at these men, I began to recognize them. They were our neighbors. They were the fathers of other children who lived on our street.

"Your husband has been molesting our children," one of the men said.

My mother shook her head in silence, denying the charge.

Another man spoke up. "Yes, he has! He's been molesting them in your garage. Our daughters have told us everything, and now we're doing something about it."

My mother took a step back from the door. The color had left her face. I think she knew that this was it. This was the moment. All of the secrets and dark lies and sinister threats and abusive behavior was being exposed right before her eyes—and mine.

"I—I don't know what you're talking about," she stammered.

"Liar!" one of them yelled. The others joined in, shouting the word at her.

As the men continued lighting into my mother, I felt a surge of vindication inside. This was what I had always wanted:

adults confronting my parents about their behavior. I had dreamed about this. Back when my first-grade teacher had suspected that something was going on, I had thought that would be the moment. But it wasn't. Little did I know that a knock at the door would be the beginning of the end for my father.

The men's voices grew louder and louder as they told my mother in no uncertain terms that they were going to call the police and have my father arrested.

As relieved as I was that this was happening, I was also growing sick to my stomach at the thought of the other children he had touched. Had he molested my friends? Who had been in my garage? What had he done to them? I thought back to all of those times when he had filmed my friends at our backyard pool parties with his home movie camera. Why had he taken such a special interest in them?

Never in my life had I imagined that he was doing this to other children. How many lives had he ruined? How many people had he destroyed?

After a few minutes, the men left. My mother closed the door slowly and didn't say a word to me. My brothers had been in their rooms, and hadn't seen the confrontation. I didn't say a word to her, because I knew there was nothing I could say. Reality had finally slammed her right in the face, and she was going to have to deal with it. I walked to my room quietly and went to bed.

The next morning, there was another knock at the front door. I watched my mother open the door and saw two policemen and a policewoman standing outside.

"Your husband has been arrested for child molestation," the policewoman told my mom.

My mother didn't react, so the policewoman repeated that my father had been arrested.

My mother seemed to come out of her daze. "But my dad is

a pastor," she said. "My dad is a pastor."

The policewoman was confused. "Ma'am, we're not talking about your dad. We are talking about your husband."

To this day, I'm not quite sure what my mother meant by that. On the one hand, it seems like she was suggesting that her father might be able to help with the situation. On the other hand, knowing what my extended family was like and how strict and unforgiving everyone was, I suppose she also may have been scared about how her father might react to all of this.

The police asked her a few more questions, took some notes, and then left. They must have arrested my father at work, I remember thinking. But he was never really in prison for what he did. It was like a furlough program. He could still go to work each day, but as I understood it, he would return to some kind of minimum detention facility at night. As I remember, after a year or two, he came back home. Back in the early '70s, these kinds of crimes just weren't dealt with the way they are today.

A few days after my father was taken in, on the way home from swim practice, we stopped at the McDonald's in Norwalk, where we often had dinner. As we were waiting in line to order our food, a man who was eating at a table started looking at us with a peculiar expression on his face.

He stood up and approached us, looking us up and down. When he finally finished studying my mother's face he raised his hand and pointed a finger at her.

"Her husband has been molesting all of your daughters!" the man shouted, so that the whole restaurant could hear him. "All of the young girls in this town were victims of her husband. Her husband is a monster. Her husband has been molesting all of our little girls!"

Immediately, the people standing near us in line started backing away. It was a busy night at the restaurant, and it felt like everyone in the place was backing away from us. There were looks of horror on everyone's faces as they stared at my mother and me and my brothers. People started saying things and yelling at my mother. It was starting to feel dangerous.

Quickly, my mother hustled us out of the restaurant and into the car. As we left the McDonald's, I can still remember the yelling of the angry mob behind us. If there had been a bunch of people with pitchforks and torches at our house that night, I would not have been surprised.

It was time for us to leave Norwalk. Thanks to my father, we were now being treated like lepers. With my dad incarcerated, my mom made plans to find a place for us to live where no one in the whole town would know who we were.

At the time, I didn't have too much time to think about all of this. I had a race coming up that would help me escape the madness. The moment I had always dreamed of—the opportunity to get away from the pain of my family—had finally arrived.

CHAPTER THREE

My First Adventure

Shortly after I turned fourteen, my coach, Flip, came over to me at practice one day and said, "Shirley, you've qualified again for the 1971 Short Course Nationals!" This one would be held that spring in Pullman, Washington.

I swam the 500-yard freestyle against the well-known swimmer Debbie Meyer, who was my hero back then. Between the ages of fourteen and eighteen, she was simply "the world's greatest female swimmer," according to the International Swimming Hall of Fame. At the 1968 Olympic Games, Debbie was the first female swimmer to win three individual gold medals at a single Olympic Games. She did so by earning the top spot in the 200, 400, and 800 freestyle events. She was named "World Swimmer of the Year" three times, and was given the James E. Sullivan Award in 1968.

I didn't know that Debbie would be retiring within just a year, at only eighteen years of age. I was a little freaked out that I was actually going to compete against her. After I did my flip turn during the 500-yard freestyle, I looked around and saw that I was actually ahead. How could this be? I was beating Debbie Meyer? That moment of realization may have cost me the race; Debbie overcame the lead and wound up winning the race. But it didn't matter. I knew I was getting better overall.

Before we left Pullman, my mom and I were both sitting on the empty bleachers surrounding the pool. I noticed that she was upset, but I didn't really understand how mad she was until she opened her mouth. "Maybe one day, you'll be able to tell your grandchildren you went to the Olympic Trials," she said to me.

I was happy with how I had done, but she sure wasn't. She was incredibly disappointed. She was suggesting that I would never get past the Olympic Trials (which would be held the following year in advance of the Munich Olympics). I knew right then and there that she really had no clue about what I was as a swimmer. My times were getting better every day. With every competition, I was growing stronger. I had done well and was proud of myself, but she didn't get it. In her narrow-minded view of swimming, if you hadn't won, you had failed. She had no concept of the growth curve that I was beginning to experience. I was swimming so well, but she couldn't see any of it.

After swimming in Pullman, I started hearing about international trips that the best swimmers got to take as part of the American team. In the back of my head, I started to put together what I would have to do to be a part of such a thing.

That summer, I qualified for the Long Course Nationals, which were to be held in Houston. My mom and I flew down there together, and I was entered in all four distances in the freestyle races.

I swam very well in my first couple of races. The next day, there was a knock on our hotel room door. My mom opened it, and there was my coach, Flip. He came into our room and sat down in a chair by the desk.

"Okay, so here's what's happening," he said, calm as usual. "Shirley can make the international team. All she needs to do tomorrow is get either first or second place in the 100 or, if she wins the 1,500, that will do it, too."

He turned to me. "How do you want to do it, Shirley? What do you want to swim?"

In my head, the decision was easy. Swimming the 100, I would have two chances to make it onto the international team. I told this to Flip, and he agreed that it was the way to go.

There was just one problem. "I know Shirley doesn't have a passport," Flip said to my mother. "We'll have to take care of that, because I really think she's going to make this team. Their plane leaves for Europe the day after the race, so we have to get the passport today. We've got a plane ticket for her to fly over to New Orleans this afternoon with another swimmer. He needs a passport, too, and they'll get that done and then fly right back to Texas."

So that's what we did. One of the coaches dropped us off at the airport and pushed our tickets into our hands, and we headed off to New Orleans—me, just fourteen years old, and this boy who was a few years older and didn't seem too thrilled about having to take a plane ride with me. He wouldn't talk to me or even look at me, while I followed him around like a little puppy.

The whole trip was such a blur. We landed in the Crescent City and took a taxi to the passport office. When I think about it today, it seems kind of crazy that they would just let us go get passports on our own. But that's just how it was back then. Nobody made a big deal out of it at all. It was just like, go get your passports and get back as fast as possible. Someone had called ahead to the passport office to let them know we were coming, so at least they were waiting for us. The boy got his passport, no problem. But I didn't have an ID, and it seemed like that was going to be an issue.

We were sitting in this hot, cramped office, waiting and waiting. The air was so incredibly thick down there, both outside and inside, and the two of us just sat there perspiring like a couple of animals. We watched the clock on the wall tick and tick and tick for more than an hour. Finally, the man who was helping us came back into the room with a smile on his face. He was holding a passport with my name and face on it.

"You're a lucky little lady," he said to me. "I didn't think you were going to be leaving with this today. This required some really special help. You have no idea how far up the ladder we had to go to get your passport. This had to be approved by someone very important."

"Who had to approve it? " I asked.

"The president," he said.

"The president of what?" I asked.

"The United States," he told me.

I had no idea if Nixon had in fact been consulted. I just knew that I finally had a passport, and now the glum teenage boy and I could head back to the airport.

We arrived safely back in Texas, and I went to bed dreaming about a chance at that international team. This was it, I thought. This was a chance to be a part of something really special and see places around the world that I'd only heard about in school. Before leaving for New Orleans, I had heard somebody say that the team was going to Russia. Just the word "Russia" seemed like another planet to me. Given my heritage, I was especially curious.

This kind of trip was beyond my wildest imagination. It was hard to fall asleep at night, just thinking about the possibilities. I didn't want to get too far ahead of myself, though. I still had to make the team.

The next day, I couldn't wait to get to the pool. I packed my bag before we left the hotel because, either way, I was headed someplace else after the races. It was either going to be home, or the other side of the world.

There was plenty of rain that day, including one monsoon cloud that parked itself right above our heads at the pool. It rained just about as hard as I've ever seen in my life. All of the swimmers and coaches were running around, freaking out over the sheets of water pouring down. But Flip said to me, "Shirley, just ignore the weather and focus on what you have to do. Just focus. You can do this."

The storm ended after a while, but everybody was still talking about the rain. In my head I was thinking, how can they not be thinking about their races right now? Why are they getting so obsessed with a thunderstorm? I knew where my head was. I was thinking about water, but not the stuff coming down from the sky. All I was concerned about was the water in the swimming pool and how long it would take me to swim through it.

At one point, while Flip was giving me my rubdown, he noticed an overhanging tarp that had filled with water and looked about ready to give way. "Let's move over a bit," he said. Moments later, it crashed down, dumping gallons of water right where I had been standing. An omen?

When it was time for my race, I was on edge. There was so much at stake here, more than I had ever been swimming for. When the starting gun went off, I knew that I had made a decent start, but after that there was no way to know how I was doing. The 100 is so crazy and there is so much splashing that it's hard to tell what's happening. I had a sick feeling that I was not in the top two, and when I touched the wall at the end, I was all but sure that I had come in third. I was so sick to my stomach that I couldn't even look at the scoreboard.

Oh well, I thought, there would be other times. At least, I hoped there would be.

When I saw Flip running over to me, I appreciated that he was smiling and that he was there to cheer me up. He was that kind of guy.

Flip knelt down by the edge of the pool and said, "You did it, Shirley. You got second place. You made the team."

I had actually done it.

That night, my mom said goodbye to me and gave me twenty dollars of spending money. I'd never had that much money in my pocket. I think she was happy for me. I mean, I hoped that she was happy for me. The hard part was that I couldn't tell her I was going to miss her, because I wasn't. I was just so happy to be spreading my wings and getting away from my parents.

Still, I gave her a hug and a kiss goodbye, and then off I went the next morning on the bus with twenty-six other swimmers, three coaches, and two chaperones.

We would be visiting Russia, East Germany, West Germany, and Denmark, among other places. As the plane rumbled down the runway and we lifted off from Houston, my mind began dreaming about what it would be like. I knew we'd be swimming over there, but I was more intrigued with the idea of travel and exploration. What would it be like? What would the people sound like? This was going to be so exciting.

On the plane we also learned that we were all going to receive a "per diem." I had no idea what that was. Gary Hall, who I swam with at the Huntington Beach Aquatic Club, explained it to me.

"It's spending money, Shirley," he said. "We are given spending money each day."

"For what?" I asked.

"Whatever you want," he said.

To me, that was simply the coolest thing ever. Gary was such a doll and I really appreciated how he kind of looked after me on that trip. He was a few years older and had already won a silver medal at the 1968 Olympic Games in Mexico City for his second place finish in the 400-meter individual medley. Two years after that, he broke the world record in the 200-meter butterfly. I was just so impressed by him.

Before getting to Russia, we stopped over at Shannon Airport in Ireland. I distinctly remember seeing all of the wonderful green colors of the country as our plane gently descended through the wispy clouds. Throughout the flight, most of the swimmers had been chatting and giggling and gossiping together. But I just sat by the window, quietly soaking in the trip.

We didn't linger in Ireland. When we landed, I had my first taste of having to run through airport terminals in a crazy rush to make a connecting flight, which would happen a lot with the swim teams I traveled with. We found our connection, took off, and soon landed in Russia or, as it was called then, the USSR.

After disembarking in Moscow, we were whisked away into a debriefing room and a stern Russian official explained to us how we were to behave in Russia and any other communist country that we happened to be visiting. With a scowl on his face, he explained to all of us through his thick accent, "You are not to take anything from any of the hotels. Not a towel. Not an ashtray. Not a pen. Do you understand? Nothing. And you are never to say anything about communism, anywhere. You don't talk about communism in your hotel room or on the elevator. There will be somebody listening to you at all times, and we will know if you break this rule."

Finally, we were admonished to not wear any revealing clothing, including shorts. And with that, we checked in at the Rossiya Hotel.

The Rossiya was a massive, five-star international hotel

that at the time was registered in *The Guinness Book of World Records* as the largest hotel in the world. (It would be surpassed by the Excalibur in Las Vegas in 1990, but it remained the largest hotel in Europe until it closed in 2006.) The place just went on forever. It was twenty-one stories high and had 3,200 rooms, 240 suites, a post office, a health club, a nightclub, a movie theater, a barbershop, and even a police station with jail cells behind unmarked black doors. It was massive, and we had a fun time exploring it. We couldn't talk about communism, but at least we were free to wander a little bit and absorb some of the atmosphere.

I was pinching myself; I was so excited to be there. I just couldn't believe that I was wandering around a giant hotel in Russia. Our first night there, we had dinner in the hotel's main dining room, and I had my first taste of real European bread. It was one of the most wonderful things I had ever tasted. All crusty on the outside and so fresh, as if it had been taken from an oven only moments beforehand (I'm sure it had been).

Just about every one of us ordered steak. I remember thinking, wow, if the bread was that good, the meat is probably going to be out of this world. But we ended up getting what looked like a healthy slab of beef liver, and most of us went back to eating the bread.

I'll never forget spending that first night in our spacious room. There were two swimmers in each room. The first thing I noticed were the blankets on the beds. They were just like the ones I had at home: comforters enveloped in comforter covers. Everyone else was saying how cool the blankets were, and I nonchalantly told them that I had the same thing at home. The other swimmers looked at me kind of funny, as if they didn't believe me.

Within just a day or so, we were slated to swim against the USSR team in Minsk. We all piled into the bus and made the trip over to the pool. On the way there, I have to admit that I wasn't too happy. Since I had qualified for the team by swimming the 100, I figured I would be swimming the 100-meter freestyle on this team. But the coaches thought it was a fluke that I'd made the team. They decided to put in another girl they thought had a better chance of winning. As for me, they were going to put me in an outside lane. I'd be swimming along in the race just for the experience; my lane wouldn't count.

Our bus pulled up to the ancient-looking swimming facility, and we all piled off and got ready for the meet. When it came time for the 100, there was little doubt in my mind that I was going to win. In fact, I led the entire way. But of course, even though I came in first, none of it counted. The girl who swam in my place technically came in second after me, but officially, she was first.

There was a lavish ceremony that night to give out the awards. I watched the other girl receive her first-place Russian crystal bowl along with ornately carved Russian nesting dolls and a huge bouquet of red roses, and I grew irritated. I thought that it should've been me up there. Little did I know that this was, in a sense, preparing me for the future.

That night, I missed Flip terribly. He never would have let something like this happen. But that's one thing I learned about the international teams: your coaches don't go along with you. You're automatically thrown into a new group of coaches that have their own style and strategy, and it doesn't always work out the way you want it to.

I chalked it up to a learning experience, and got back to enjoying the trip. The good news was that the coaches were re-thinking things after seeing how I swam. "Okay, Shirley," one of them said, almost begrudgingly, "you will now swim in the official races." From then on, I never swam in a practice lane again.

After Minsk, we went back to Moscow, where we would

have some free time. We saw the Kremlin and St. Basil's Cathedral. We also saw a round, raised cement circle. When we asked
what it was, our guide said, "It's where they used to chop people's heads off." We saw the building that housed Lenin's body,
called Lenin's Mausoleum, in Red Square. We also went into a
huge and well-known department store called GUM, where I
was elbowed out of way by aggressive Russian shoppers. Moscow was fascinating, and I loved visiting there.

Next, it was on to Denmark, and then Amsterdam.

The red light district in Amsterdam was unlike anything
I had ever seen before. There were storefronts that stretched
three to four blocks long, and in each window was a different
girl that could be had for the evening. Behind the glass, they
would be doing various things—knitting, reading, or even just
sitting there watching television. There were strange aromas in
the air and everyone on the team stared wide-eyed at all the various illicit trade taking place around us. Our chaperones didn't
let us linger there, though. We were just sightseers, stumbling
upon new places to explore. It was all kind of vague and mysterious to me, and as wild as it was, it represented something
that seemed so exotic. This is what people see when they travel,
I remember thinking to myself.

While in Amsterdam, I had the opportunity to swim against
Enith Brigitha, who would become the first black athlete to win
a swimming medal at the Olympics the following year. Swimming against her in a twenty-five-meter pool, I didn't do very
well. But it was okay. I was still adjusting to the travel and the
different settings.

The European pools, in general, were very different than
the American pools. They were very old and there was no smell
of chlorine. It's funny; I kind of missed the smell of chlorine
because it reminded me of the pools back home.

I really loved West Germany. It was so beautiful, clean, and colorful. The smells that flowed through the air were all incredible. Restaurants, bakeries, cheese shops, flower shops, chocolate shops, coffee shops—I could live here, I thought to myself.

While West Germany reminded me of a Disneyland attraction, East Germany was something else altogether. We didn't swim there—we just took a brief tour, entering through a place called Checkpoint Charlie. At age fourteen, I didn't know what that was, but I'd heard my brother use the term while playing the card game War. Checkpoint Charlie was, in fact, just an unassuming guardhouse that was the main demarcation point between Allied-occupied West Berlin and Soviet-held East Berlin. It acted as a way station for officials (or visitors like us) traveling from one side of the Wall to the other. Soldiers came onto the bus and thoroughly looked through our passports. I wasn't scared, but I had the feeling that they didn't like the idea of us being there.

Entering the country was like watching *The Wizard of Oz* in reverse. Everything went from vivid colors to bleak black and white and gray. In East Berlin, the sky was gray. The buildings were gray. The people were gray huddled masses, all holding umbrellas in the drizzling rain. They walked with their heads pointed down at the ground and shoulders slumped. It was depressing and joyless. Luckily, we didn't stay long. There was nothing to do and nothing to see. To be honest, I don't even know why we went there, other than to say we visited.

Back in West Germany, we swam some practices at Baden-Baden, a spa town on the fringe of the Black Forest. The pools there, located in a forested park, seemed ancient and mysterious to me.

From there, it was on to West Berlin, Bremen, Frankfurt, and, finally, Munich. I think Munich may have been the most special place of all the cities we visited. We were given a special tour at the construction site of the next Olympic Games, which would be taking place in just one year. It was remarkable what was being built there. The grounds were simply beautiful, and the facilities looked stunning.

Standing in the nearly empty Olympic Village, I wandered away from my teammates and took all of it in. I thought to myself, I will be back here next year. No matter what, I have to make it back here next year.

CHAPTER FOUR

A New Coach

When I returned to the U.S. from Europe in July 1971, it was like coming back to a new life. My mother had packed up the family and moved to Fountain Valley—which is right next to Huntington Beach, where I swam—and I was about to start my sophomore year at Fountain Valley High School without knowing a single person. I was already missing all of the freedom I'd had while traveling abroad with the team.

As we settled into our new life in Fountain Valley, I was swimming more than ever, constantly thinking about the '72 Games in Munich. Did I really have a shot? My coach, Flip, seemed to think so, and he was going to make sure that I trained the way Olympians do: frequently and intensely. I was already swimming two-and-a-half-hour practices with him after school every day at the Huntington Beach Aquatic Club, but he felt I needed another session built into the day to get where I needed to be. Since the pool we used in the afternoon was booked in the morning, he found another twenty-five-yard pool in nearby Garden Grove where we could have access.

These extra practices required me to get up very early in the morning, but I had no problem with that. I was very determined and extremely competitive and, most importantly, I trusted Flip with everything. When he told me to arrive at the pool every morning at 5:30, I was always there on time. He would work with me for an hour and a half, and then I would go home, get changed, and go to school. I did this every single day.

Flip thought it would be a good idea for me to wear a sweatshirt in the water for the first half of my evening practices. That would create an artificial lag, which would force me to swim harder. The sweatshirt was really heavy, so we compromised and I cut the sleeves off. Now when I swam against the others, I wasn't as far ahead of them as I usually was. But I wasn't behind, either; just in the middle.

There were other training techniques Flip used on all of us that made the whole team stronger. He tied surgical tubing to the aluminum bleachers at Golden West College, which he attached to belts that we wore around our waists. We would then swim out as far as we could and strain to swim against the taut tubing. We would end up swimming in one place for about a minute or two, but it was one of the most intense exercises we would ever do.

Puffing on his ever-present pipe, Flip also took us outside to do exercises on the grass. Sit-ups, flutter kicks, leg lifts— and then back into the water. And, of course, we all used his famous paddles in the water. Modeled after paddles invented by Benjamin Franklin, Flip's paddles were plastic rectangles that we strapped onto our hands with surgical tubing. The paddles increased the surface area of your hands, making it harder to push through the water. Those things are still one of the most effective tools for becoming a stronger swimmer. You have to remember that Flip was a true innovator when it came to coaching. He had already helped the careers of many champions, and was a legend at that point. I'm not sure everyone on the team appreciated just how good he was.

When I think back on it today, this was the time when I was really on my way, though I didn't know it at the time. But Flip did. He could see my future, and he was doing everything he could to help me realize it.

Each day, as I swam my laps at the Huntington Beach Aquatic Club, Flip would walk alongside me on the deck, smiling as he said in a singsong sort of voice: "Shane Gould . . . Shane Gould . . . " It was his way of pushing me, taunting me with the name of the famed Aussie swimmer.

Flip also taught me an important strategy called negative splitting. It's something that runners do, too. Basically, it means that you start slow and finish fast. For instance, if you are swimming a 400-meter freestyle and you explode right at the beginning, you will get tired around the 200 mark. With negative splitting, you take it pretty easy until you hit 200. Then, when everyone else is basically dying in the water, you'll be ready to just take over. Flip was a really big fan of this strategy.

For the next nine months, this was my life: morning sessions with Flip, school, and then practicing with my team in Huntington Beach. I felt myself getting stronger and more competitive every day. I mean, I've been competitive since I was little kid. But as a fifteen-year-old, it was getting really intense. I hated losing. Winning was all that mattered.

In 1972, I swam in various meets and made the time standards for the Olympic Trials in the 100, 200, and 400 freestyles. By the time the Trials rolled around, I was feeling really good. Flip had been pumping me up for months.

When it finally came time to pack up and head to Chicago the first week of August to compete at the Olympic Trials, I was excited. We landed at O'Hare Airport and headed straight to Portage Park in the suburbs, where the Trials would be held. There would be no sightseeing in Chicago on this four-day trip.

Once we had arrived and settled into the hotel, my mom told me, "You have a chance here to break the world record in the 200-meter freestyle. You have to be able to taste it if you're really going to do it."

Taste it? I asked myself. What does that even mean? It didn't make much sense to me, but I guess that was her way of trying to motivate me.

I came in second in the 100 and second in the 400 as well. But in the 200, I did more than taste a world record—I scored one, my very first. I broke Shane Gould's record, with a time of 2:05.21. The place went absolutely nuts. The strange thing was that it felt easy. Afterwards, I realized that I could actually have swum even faster.

That race, in my opinion, represented my arrival on the world swimming stage. Nothing ever felt the same after that 200. Now, people knew my name. Now, people seemed to be talking about me when I walked by. I knew that I was headed for the Olympics.

Flip was so excited. In his eyes, those ever-twinkling and mischievous eyes, I could see how proud he was that all of our work had paid off. Even then, at the beginning of my journey, he saw potential in me that I didn't even known was there.

The next morning, we would head off to Olympic training. As I got on the bus to go back to the hotel and pack up my things, I remember asking my mom, "Wait, those same Olympics that we watch on television? That's really what I'm going to go compete in?" She nodded her head. Flip came over and said, "Shirley, there's only one Olympics, and you'll be swimming at them." That's when it started to sink in. I was really going to the Olympics.

A reporter came over to me and said, patting me on the back, "Finally, the United States has a premier freestyler."

From Chicago I was sent to Knoxville, Tennessee, for two

weeks of training before the Olympics. I was disappointed when I learned that Flip wouldn't be going with me. It made absolutely no sense to me that a swimmer's personal coach could not come and be with them before the most important races of their lives. But back then, that's just how it was. You would be under the control of coaches you'd never met before. It was a very unsettling feeling; I'm glad that the policy has since changed.

Still, the coaches, led by Sherm Chavoor, turned out to be great. As soon as we arrived at the University of Tennessee at Knoxville, we settled into some fun, interesting practices. Sherm was older, kind of like Flip, and I liked his style. It was also beautiful in Knoxville, and I really enjoyed the fact that they gave us some time to explore the area. We even got to have dinner at the house of famous college football coach Bear Bryant.

At training camp, we ran through the 400 freestyle relay and set a world record, which we were super happy about. As we approached the end of our training, we all got fitted for our Olympic uniforms. That was so exciting. They actually picked me as the model to use in magazines to illustrate what the uniforms were going to look like. They also gave us our own USA sweatsuits and bags full of freebies like goggles, Chapstick, and sunscreen—anything you might need while swimming. Best of all, we each got our own camera, the old-fashioned kind with the flashcube that rotated with each shot you took. They wanted us to take pictures of our experiences at the Olympics, which seemed like a really nice idea.

When our training ended, we all boarded our charter plane at the airport in Knoxville, and then we were off. Next stop, Munich.

CHAPTER FIVE

Munich

I was so excited to go back to Munich. West Germany had made such a positive impression on me the year before. On the charter flight to Munich, everyone was giddy and upbeat. We had some phenomenal swimmers with us, including Mark Spitz, so we were confident.

It was amazing to me how much the Olympic Village had transformed in just one year. They had done a marvelous job. As we wandered around the Village, I could feel the other athletes' excitement building. I especially liked seeing everybody wearing their native dress. There were people from Kenya, Japan, Luxembourg, Morocco, Australia, and anyplace else you could imagine.

Probably the coolest thing, at least for me, was the fact that I got to have my own little apartment. Imagine a fifteen-year-old being given that much freedom and independence. My apartment had a little kitchenette, I got my own key, and I was totally on my own. It was like a dream.

For me, it felt more like I was on vacation than at the Olympic Games. Every day, the housekeepers left baskets of chocolate and treats in our apartments. The cafeteria in the complex was incredible. I had always liked yogurt, but it was too expensive for our family to buy every week. When I saw the yogurt bar in the cafeteria, it blew my mind. The cafeteria also served a buffet that offered the native cuisines of all the different countries participating in the Games. You could sample dishes that you never would have tasted otherwise.

The other athletes were really nice; it was easy to get along with everyone. I mostly hung out with my teammates, Jennifer Wylie and Jo Harshbarger. We were all about the same age, and they were both really fun girls. On any swimming trip, everyone gravitated toward the people they felt most comfortable with, even if it meant that little cliques formed. We had all been thrown into this crazy, gypsy-like world together, and it was natural to stay close to those you could best relate to. Age made a difference, too. The older girls tended to stay together, just as the younger girls did.

They made the experience so much fun for all of us. They had a giant chess set in the Village that was like something out of *Alice in Wonderland*, and there was even a music room where you could listen to any album you wanted to on a brand-new stereo. One night, we all went down to the music room and ABC-TV filmed me, Jo, and Jennifer singing off-key with our headphones on. I'd never had more fun in my life than I did at the Games.

Although Flip could not come along with me as an official coach at the Games, he flew to Munich on his own anyway. I was thrilled. Even though he wasn't coaching me there, just having him close by made a big difference in my mindset.

One night, the phone rang in my little apartment and I was so happy to hear Flip's voice on the other end of the line.

"Shirley," he said, "let me take you out to dinner. You've got a few days before the Games start, and it will be a good chance to talk about your races."

So that night, we took off out of the Olympic Village and went to a restaurant where he insisted I try Wiener Schnitzel for the first time. The thin, pan-fried veal cutlet was delicious.

As kind of a gimmick, someone had made t-shirts for our team that said, "All That Glitters Is Not Gould." Yeah, like that was going to psyche out Shane Gould. We all wore them at practice one day, but the reaction was not what we had expected. The fans and other teams were put off by the shirts, and I can understand why: it showed just how dominant Shane was. Great competitors feed off of that kind of thing, and we may have actually motivated her a bit by wearing those t-shirts.

As athletes at the Games, we started feeling like celebrities right away. If you were wearing your warm-up jacket, which most of us often did, there was no way to get from point A to point B without getting mobbed for autographs. One time, my friend Jo and I were trying to get some lunch when a wave of people suddenly encircled us, pushing pens and programs in our faces. Both of us had relatively long last names to write out when people asked us for autographs, so I whispered to Jo, "I think I'm just going to write Mark's name on a few of these instead. Do you think anyone will notice?"

"Do it," she laughed. "Let's see."

So I did. I started signing "Mark Spitz" from time to time just to get through the crush of people in as short a time as possible. Nobody ever seemed to notice. Sometimes I wonder if any of those autographs still exist, the rare "Shirley-Babashoff-signing-as-Mark-Spitz."

When it was time for the American teams to get ready for the opening ceremonies, it was chaotic. They had given us so many different clothing options that nobody knew what to wear. What would make us all look like a team? Which scarf should we wear? Which shoes? Which jacket? It was completely disorganized, and it took a good couple of hours to find someone in charge to make those decisions for us.

When we were all dressed, they began herding us over to the

stadium, which was within walking distance. On the way over, our team mingled with athletes from lots of other countries. It was chaos, but it was fun. I still couldn't believe I was there.

Olympiastadion was the main venue for the '72 Summer Olympic Games. It was the most impressive structure I had ever seen in my life. We all oohed and ahhed as we got closer to it. Designed by the German architect Gunther Behnisch, it featured large, sweeping canopies of acrylic glass stabilized by steel cables, which were meant to imitate the Alps and help overshadow the 1936 Summer Olympics in Berlin, held during the Nazi regime. The transparent canopy symbolized the new, democratic, and optimistic Germany, which was reflected in the Games' official motto that year: "The cheerful Games."

When we all walked in wearing our uniforms (for us girls, it was red jackets over white skirts), the crowd of almost 100,000 went nuts. Back then, everybody was happy to see the American team walk in because of everything that we stood for. I think we got the biggest reaction from the crowd out of all the teams except for, of course, the West Germans.

The show began with a speech by Avery Brundage, the president of the International Olympic Committee. After he delivered the Olympic Oath, thousands of white doves were released into the air to signify the start of the Games. One of them actually pooped on the head of a U.S. athlete, a young African American girl who was on the track and field team. Rather than freak out about it, she laughed and the press started taking pictures of her. I even got into a shot with her.

One thing people may not realize is that, during the opening ceremonies, the athletes can't see anything. Down on the field, you have no idea what the spectacle is like from up in the stands. At one point, I wondered why we were still standing there. Evidently, a huge dance show was in progress, but we couldn't see it at all.

I would be swimming in four events at the '72 Games: the 100 freestyle, the 200 freestyle, the 400 freestyle, and the 4x100 freestyle relay. Going to the Olympics, though, didn't mean that you were automatically in the finals. Everyone would compete in the "prelims," and only the top eight would make the finals in the evening.

A couple of days before the swimming events began, Olympic officials paid us a visit to pull out a strand of hair from each of our heads. They would test the hair to make sure we were actually women—a basic DNA test, I guess, but I had never heard of that before. How could there be any confusion about what sex you were? Those things were obvious, right?

On August 29, I stepped into the Olympia Schwimmhalle to compete in my very first event at the Olympics: the 100-meter freestyle. Designed with a double-curvature roof made out of a lightweight "skin," the Schwimmhalle looked both classic and futuristic at the same time. It was just gorgeous.

I did really well in the event, coming in second ahead of Shane Gould, who took the bronze. A silver medal! My teammate, Sandy Neilson, won the gold. Facing each other in the water with our lanes next to each other, we hugged before getting out of the pool.

"Excellent job, Shirley," she said to me.

We stood on the platform together and received our medals as our national anthem filled the hall. It was such a special feeling to medal in my very first Olympic event. All of the sudden, it became real: I was part of the Olympic Games that I had watched on television four years before. I was part of something big.

Before the Games, I had been told that if you came in first, second, or third, you would have to go into a little room and pee into a cup so they could test your urine for drugs. Sure enough, after I won the 100 freestyle, I was taken into that little room. They directed me to a small refrigerator and told me to find something to drink if I needed it. Inside, there were a few cans of soda and a couple of bottles of beer.

"I can have whatever I want?" I asked.

"Sure," they replied. "Take anything you want."

Feeling a little daring, I grabbed one of the beers and knocked it back. I was in a bold mood after winning my first medal. I'd had beer at family functions before, so it was nothing new to me. When I was taken into the room after winning my second and third medals later in the Games, I opened the refrigerator door and looked for another beer, but there weren't any. Some of the other swimmers must have had the same idea that I did.

The next day, August 30, was the 400-meter freestyle event. Early that morning, I was sitting in one of the grandstands with Flip. As we sat together in the quiet stands, he looked at me with a smile that said he was up to something. That was Flip. It was like he had a secret that nobody else knew. Holding his trademark pipe in one hand, he spoke to me quietly.

"Okay, Shirley," he said. "I think the 400 is the place to try the negative split."

That caught me off guard. It wasn't a bad idea, but we hadn't discussed it at all before this. But I had such faith in Flip that I bought into the idea right away.

Mastering the negative split was very tough. You had to decide at what point you would really kick things in, so no two races were ever the same. But Flip was confident that I could do it.

"Remember, you're basically swimming two 200s," he explained. "The first one is a warm-up. Keep loose after you dive in. I know you're going to want to explode and take the lead right away, but hold back. Relax as best you can."

He knew how competitive I was, and how hard it would be to not go off at the gun and try to end the race right there. But he also knew better than I did, and there was no way I was going to challenge him on this.

"Once you start catching up," he continued, "the leaders are going to see you gaining and psychologically that's going to be very tough for them. They're going to know how tired they are and they're going to realize how fresh you are, and that's how you can win this race."

So, when the race started later that day, as tough as it was to not go all out, I hung back. Holding back was against my nature, but I understood the strategy and I trusted it. When I made my move, I knew I had a shot to win the race. The only problem was, I started to speed up just a little bit too late. I had tons of energy and speed left in me, but I hadn't given myself enough time to catch up to the leaders.

Shane Gould took the gold in the 400 and I came in fourth, barely missing the bronze medal. But I was happy. I had swum my best time ever in the 400 and took it as a learning experience. From that moment on, I understood how to control the back end of the negative split. It was all just learning.

After the race, Flip came down to the deck to visit with a smile on his face. He gave me a hug and told me that I had done great. I looked up at him and said, "Flip, I wasn't even tired at the end of that race." He smiled and said, "I know."

August 30 was also the day of the 400 freestyle relay. It had been eight years since any nation other than the United States had set a world record in the event. Sandy Neilson, Jennifer Kemp, Jane Barkman, and I had practiced the race back in Knoxville, and we'd set a world record in that pool. We were pretty sure we were going to take the gold on this day. But I was just fifteen years old—a kid—and I was just excited to go out and give it my all.

At practice a couple of days before the relay, our coach had pulled me aside. "Shirley," he said, "you're going to swim anchor. I like what you've been doing here in Munich, and I think you'll finish strong for us. You're a sprinter, and we're going to really need that at the end."

Wow. Anchor. I had always loved the idea of swimming fourth, because it felt like it was you winning the race if your team finished first. The most exciting part of a relay event was the end, when the anchors went at it. That was where the winners were often determined.

Sandy Neilson, who had won our gold the day before, led off the final for our team. Our coach had explained to her that he was letting her lead off to give her a shot at a world record. It's a little-know fact that in swimming, the first leg of the relay begins with a starting gun, or a "dead start," so they can actually get a world record time in the record books. The second, third, and fourth legs cannot be counted as individual world record times, because the swimmers anticipate their leaps into the water.

Almost immediately, Sandy put us ahead. But on the second leg, East Germany's Andrea Eife pulled even with our swimmer, Jenny. After the third leg, which Jane swam, the race was still a dead heat. Then it was time for me, the anchor, to dive in. I would be swimming against Kornelia Ender from East Germany. One day, we would become great rivals under very controversial circumstances. But that was a long way off.

In this race, it was tight from the get-go. I got a good jump off the blocks, but Ender and I were neck and neck for most of the first length. Then I did what I still think was one of the worst flip turns I'd ever done in my life. Just awful, and it allowed Ender to take the lead coming home. The crowd started going crazy as she and I battled it out, but it was starting to slip away. I could hear Flip's voice in my head, coaching me, telling me to be strong and swim my race. I knew I was dead if I lost this race for our team.

Then the adrenaline kicked in. I pushed like never before. Sorry, Kornelia. Sorry, East Germany. Not today.

I beat Kornelia, and we won the gold medal. We set a world record that day, at 3:55:19. It was an amazing feeling, being hugged by teammates and hearing the crowd go crazy. The real shock that day was watching Australia—with Shane Gould—finish last. I looked over my teammates' shoulders as we hugged and celebrated, and I saw Shane's face. Looking at her, I could tell that something had changed. Oh, she'd done well overall. Very well, in fact. She'd won three gold medals and set a world record in each race. She'd also won a silver and a bronze. Still, after the relay race, her face looked empty.

Everyone had expected us to take that gold medal, but it was still a very special feeling to finish the way we did and hear the crowd cheer us on. At just fifteen years old, I had anchored a race and helped win a gold medal for my country. I felt very proud.

It was an amazing feeling to stand on the gold podium and hear our national anthem again. Back home, I knew that my family was watching. Someone had lent them a color TV just for the event.

Beating Kornelia Ender for the gold in the relay would one day prove to be prophetic. She was a pretty good swimmer. That East German team was good. I heard some people talking about how much they had improved. I had no prior experience competing against them, but they started turning heads at the '72 Games.

Next for me was the 200-meter freestyle, on September 1. Shane Gould had set two world records in this event in 1971, and I had beaten both of them at the Olympic Trials in Chicago the month before. Shane took the lead against me almost immediately and, at 100 meters, was half a body length ahead of me and my teammates, Keena Rothhammer and Ann Marshall. I knew that I should have picked up my pace a little earlier than I had. You couldn't hang back too long against someone as good as Shane Gould. In a distance event, you can usually sneak a peek at the clock while you're taking a breath and when I did that, I knew I had blown it. I was still learning how to manage the clock. Keena and I would both better the Chicago world record, but it would only be good for the silver and bronze medals, respectively, as Gould shattered the mark for the gold with 2:03.56.

When I got out of the pool, Flip was right there for me on the deck.

"You should be proud, Shirley," he said. "You're learning a lot out there. I can tell. This is all about learning for you right now. Figuring things out. Your first Olympics, and you're swimming like a champ. And you just won another silver medal!"

As much fun as I was having at the Olympics, a major highlight was watching Mark Spitz swim at the Games. I mean, I knew he was a remarkable individual. He'd already had quite the amateur swimming career. In 1967, he had won five gold medals at the Pan American Games, setting a record that lasted until 2007. By the time the 1968 Olympics rolled around, he was already the holder of ten world records. At those Games, with very high hopes surrounding him, he won just two gold medals, one in the 4x100-meter freestyle relay and the other in the 4x200-meter freestyle relay. The next year, he enrolled at Indiana University and trained with the famous swimming coach Doc Counsilman, who had also coached Mark at the '68 Games. As a Hoosier, Mark won eighteen individual NCAA titles. In 1971, he was given the James E. Sullivan Award as the top amateur athlete in the United States. He also set a few world records during the Olympic Trials in Chicago that I actually got to witness.

"Mark the Shark," everybody called him. He was seven years older than me at the '72 Games, so to me, he really seemed like an adult even though he was only twenty-two years old. He was naturally sort of lanky; I'd always thought that he had the absolute perfect swimmer's body for the butterfly and freestyle. He also had a little patch of whitish hair on the back of his head. People would always say, "Hey Mark, did you rub up against some wet paint?" You could tell that he got tired of hearing the same question over and over.

I think a lot of us knew that Mark had something special in store for Munich, but we didn't realize just how special it would be. Watching him swim in Munich, I was in awe. He had perfect form. With each first-place finish, you knew something special was happening. By the time he won his seventh gold, I realized that I was watching real history take place. He was a superstar. The crowd adored him, and everybody on our team was so proud of him.

When Michael Phelps broke Mark's record in 2008 by winning eight gold medals at the Beijing Olympics, someone asked me how I compared those two phenomenal swimmers. For me, it was an easy answer. Michael Phelps was obviously at the top of his game and a brilliant competitor, but he was also a professional. He had a lot of support and backing and many other things that amateur athletes didn't have in the early '70s. For him, swimming was his career. For Mark in 1972, swimming was simply his sport. He didn't get paid for it; he did it purely for the love of swimming and competition. To me, there's a huge difference. When I say that, I don't mean to undermine Michael at all; he's an incredible swimmer. But it should certainly make you appreciate what Mark accomplished in the early '70s, given the circumstances. In those days, nobody ever planned on making money from competing in the Olympics. Of course, given Mark's success, he was able to turn it into a career afterward. But while he was swimming, he wasn't afforded any of the luxuries that the best swimmers in the world have today.

Watching Mark at the 1972 Olympics, when swimming was one of the most popular sports on the planet, was probably the most breathtaking thing I have ever witnessed. As Mark swam the 100-meter freestyle, I remember hearing that he may have been vulnerable after already winning five gold medals. One of Mark's teammates, Jerry Heidenreich, was a strong swimmer; we heard that the race would be close between them. Mark had started out fast and reached the turn well ahead of Jerry, but Jerry came on strong in the end. For a moment, I thought Mark's streak might have been broken, but he held on and won the gold. What a privilege it was to watch someone like Mark. Pure inspiration.

A couple of days later, on September 5, I wandered over to the Village cafeteria by myself to get breakfast. When I got to the check-in kiosk, I could tell that something was different. For starters, there were no autograph hounds wandering around, waiting for the athletes. Even stranger, there was a phalanx of soldiers armed with machine guns lining the perimeter of the entrance.

What was going on?

The television sets in our apartments only broadcasted the Games on a closed circuit; we didn't have any news channels. We had no idea that a tragedy was taking place at that very moment.

A journalist came over to me and said, "If you have your ID, they will still let you in." I asked him if he knew what was going on, but he just shook his head and quickly walked away.

Inside, the cafeteria was like a ghost town. I ran into a couple of other American athletes who didn't know was going on, either. We heard some murmurs from people about a problem over on the men's side of the Village, but not much more than that.

All of the sudden, I wasn't hungry anymore. I went back to my apartment with my best swimming pal at that time, Jo Harshbarger. "Come on," she said. "Let's go see Mark. I think he's leaving."

Mark Spitz was leaving the Olympics? He was the star of the Games, having won seven gold medals. Leaving? That didn't make any sense. We set off to find him.

When we got to his apartment, he was all packed up and was being hustled out of the lobby by a bunch of security guards. We caught his eye and he just shrugged and said, "See ya."

As I would soon learn, because Mark was Jewish, he was now a marked man at the '72 Olympic Games.

We all went back to our complex. Once there, our chaperones explained a little bit about what was happening, but in vague terms.

"There's a problem," one of them said. "Some very bad people with guns have disrupted the Games and for our own safety, we are not allowed to leave the Village. Not to worry—you're all safe."

The mystery of what was happening created a sort of nervous giddiness among many of the girls. We didn't know enough details to be all that scared, but we could tell something big was happening. And it was kind of creepy how the overall mood of the place had changed so quickly. But how to pass the time?

For starters, a bunch of the girls dragged their mattresses

over to my apartment and we huddled together, laying low until the storm cleared. We all sat together and imagined what might be happening on the outside. It reminded me of telling ghost stories around a campfire. At one point, Jennifer Wylie crept over to the window, looked back at us with an alarmed expression on her face, and said, "Someone is coming up the balcony to get us!" Soon after, another girl said, "Wait, listen, I hear someone trying to get in through the ceiling tiles!" We all shrieked and laughed. We were just teenage girls, trying to make light of a clearly serious situation to ease the tension.

The next day, our chaperones left the Village to fly back home, and our team was on its own. Thinking about this today, it's incredible that we had no real adult supervision, given what was going on. But the times were very different. A teammate told me that a few of the other girls were taking a train trip to Austria to explore. "We should go!" she said. So we hopped on a train to Salzburg with a few of the other girls and spent the day sightseeing and visiting places where *The Sound of Music* had been filmed. I loved the castles and the old cathedrals. Being from Southern California, they reminded me of Fantasyland at Disneyland, but much bigger.

The trip was a wonderful escape from the doom and gloom at the Olympic Village, but as night crept in across the mountains and we caught the last train back, we started to understand the full scope and seriousness of what had happened. There was a daily newspaper printed for the athletes called the *Village News*, and once we got back to our apartments, we all started to look over the issues from the last couple of days. It was very disturbing. All of the shoe companies, like Adidas and Puma, had taken out ads in the daily paper expressing their sorrow and frustration.

The next day, there was a memorial service for the athletes who had been killed. That's when it really hit all of us. It was devastating. We learned about the Black September faction of the Palestine Liberation Organization, and how they had brought duffel bags loaded with assault rifles, pistols, and grenades to the Games to ambush the Israeli athletes. To this day, the Munich massacre overshadows everything that happened at those Games, including the amazing accomplishments of my teammate, Mark Spitz. Those terrible events sucked away all of the joy and happiness that so many people had experienced. It was gut-wrenching.

Piling back onto the chartered plane to head back home, our whole team was numb. Unlike our boisterous flight to the Games, this flight was silent. We landed at JFK Airport in New York and then went our separate ways to our hometowns. A bunch of us boarded a plane to California, but even on that flight, the mood was somber. It was not at all the ending we had imagined.

CHAPTER SIX

Feeling Like a Celebrity

I'd had my first taste of the Olympics, and I knew I wanted-ed more. As competitive as I was, I realized that there was no greater stage to be swimming on. When I got home, I decided that I was going to devote every minute of every day to making the team so I could swim in the Montreal Olympics in 1976.

Our families and friends were waiting for us at the airport in Los Angeles, and there were some reporters and photographers, too. There were plenty of hugs, bouquets of flowers, and even some tears. My mom was there, stoic and impassive as usual, to collect me and drive me home once I'd grabbed my bags off the luggage carousel. When I arrived back at my house, things were pretty much as I had left them.

I entered my junior year within days of getting home. The very first day of school, I was summoned to the principal's office. What did I do now? Did I forget my lunch?

When I got to the principal's office, I saw my mother waiting for me there and I panicked a bit. This must be really bad if she's here, I thought.

But then I saw the principal, Dr. Paul Berger, and he had a big smile on his face. "Shirley, we are so proud of you!" he exclaimed. "We all watched you in the Olympics and would love for you to go out and speak to the entire student body today.

Isn't that exciting?"

Actually, for me, no. I was very shy and withdrawn, and I also happened to attend the largest public high school in the United States, with over 4,500 students enrolled that year.

Moments later, I was standing onstage in front of a microphone. The crowd looked like an entire city of people to me; they were screaming and photographers were taking pictures of me. I had no idea what to say, but I managed to get a few words out about what it felt like to win medals at the Olympics. I remember saying at one point that "it was really clean over there."

Someone asked me what it was like to hear the famous Olympic musical theme when I received my medals. I replied that you actually never even hear that song when you win; they just use it for the television broadcast. When I left school that day, I saw on the marquee outside the school that it had been proclaimed "Shirley Babashoff Day."

The next day, the *Los Angeles Times* ran a photo of me giving my speech in front of a giant American flag. This is exciting, I thought. I'd never thought about what it might be like to become a celebrity. But all of the sudden, people treated me differently. My mom and I would be in the supermarket and I would notice other mothers pointing at me and whispering to their children. At five-foot-seven, with short, spiky hair and terrible self-esteem, I was self-conscious and always assumed that they were saying bad things about me.

But then I would listen and find that the moms were actually singing my praises. They were telling their children, "That's Shirley Babashoff. She won three medals at the Olympics, and she's one of the best swimmers in America." It made me feel really good.

One day when I got home from school, I found my mom in the kitchen holding an envelope. She was just staring at it, kind of tracing the return address with her forefinger.

"I think you should open this," she said.

"Is everything okay?" I asked.

"I hope so," she said. "This is from the White House."

I carefully opened the envelope and read the letter inside.

Dear Miss Babashoff,

All of America joins me in welcoming you home from the 1972 Summer Olympics. Your gold and two silver medals are splendid tributes not only to your skill as a swimmer but, perhaps more importantly, to your dedication to the ideals of the Olympic tradition. On behalf of your fellow citizens, I am delighted to extend my heartiest congratulations to you for the honor you have brought to yourself and to your country.

With my best wishes,
Sincerely,
Richard Nixon

Wow, I thought. That's pretty cool. A signed letter from the president of the United States. The same guy who supposedly made it possible for me to get my passport in New Orleans when I had made my first European trip the year before. Despite all of the horrible things that had happened in Munich, the entire experience had been like a dream come true. I'd never had more fun in my life, and it had set me on a definite course for the next four years. And the president was congratulating me? I was just thankful for the privilege of being able to go over there and do what I did.

As I was standing there, basking in the glow of the letter, my mother walked over to me and plucked it out of my hands. She stuck it back in the envelope and tucked it away in a special box where she kept souvenirs from my swimming career thus far.

For those first couple of months, I went back to my normal life, if you can call it that. There was a big parade for some of us athletes at Disneyland, and I was honored in a parade right in Fountain Valley. It was kind of fun being a celebrity. Articles about me popped up in the papers, too. In one of them, somebody described me as "the leggy steelworker's daughter with apple pie good looks."

As far as swimming, I was still practicing at Golden West every day and working hard during my junior year. One day, shortly after returning to the pool, my teammates and I received a letter from Flip telling us that he was retiring from coaching. This was a huge blow for all of us, but for me it was a real devastation. Flip had been a remarkably powerful force in my life, and I was heartbroken when he made the decision to stop coaching.

As tough as it was, we still had to figure something out. Most of us on the team basically had two options: swim at Belmont Shore or head down to Mission Viejo, where a club called the Nadadores was making a real name for itself on weekends at Mission Viejo High School and the Marguerite Aquatic Center. The team had been founded in 1968, and today holds the record for winning the most team titles at the U.S. Swimming Nationals. Over the years, many well-known swimmers and divers have been Nadadores, including Greg Louganis and Dara Torres.

When my teammates and I carpooled down there to check them out, we were slightly nervous. The little bit we knew about the team involved their coach, Mark Schubert, who reportedly ran brutal practices. Rumor had it that his kids were swimming 15,000 meters a day; we were used to 8,500.

Mark's first coaching job had been in 1972, at Cuyahoga Falls High School in Ohio. He had recently become the head coach at Mission Viejo. In the thirteen years that followed, his teams would win a total of forty-four national championship titles.

We all met Mark, and we liked him. Unlike Flip, he wasn't that much older than me. He struck me as very cool—especially when he pulled up in his powder-blue Porsche. And the pool and overall facilities were just gorgeous. We took part in a couple of practices and they didn't seem that different from what we had been doing.

I transferred down to Mission Viejo to work with Mark, along with five others from my Huntington Beach team. Within just a few weeks, our practices stretched to about 15,000 meters a day, or more. Mark had been shrewd enough to go easy on us at first. A couple of my teammates dropped out, but most of us stuck with it. We were young, so as much swimming as that was, we could adapt pretty quickly to the new rigors of Mark's sessions.

My new schedule was pretty brutal. I got up at 4:30 AM to head down to Mission Viejo High School for a two-hour practice before coming back home to get ready for school. After school, from 5:00 PM to 8:00 PM, I was back down in Mission Viejo for another practice. Each practice session usually involved swimming about ten miles, so for me, that came out to twenty miles a day, total. For the four years that followed, that's what I did every day without fail.

Back then, swimming was much more popular than it is now. Mission Viejo was quickly becoming the swimming Mecca of California, and when you consider that California was the swimming Mecca of the United States, then that really meant something.

Mark and I got along right away. He was tough and intense, but I liked him. He managed literally hundreds of swimmers throughout the entire program, but he obviously paid special attention to people like me, Brian Goodell, and several others. I

loved that Mark did not allow parents anywhere near the swimming pool. Over the years, I had grown tired of my mother's
constant presence at practice. I didn't like having her there.
Watching her sit there with a stopwatch, keeping my times . . . it
just seemed so unnecessary, especially as I grew older. She didn't
really understand how the practices worked, and she never understood the strategy of swimming for time, pacing, tapering,
or even winding down. She'd just keep time and assume that
you always had to be going your fastest, no matter what.

For all of the strengths that I exhibited in the water, I definitely had some weak spots, too, and Mark knew it. I will admit, my turns were always a lot slower and not as efficient as
a lot of other swimmers. I used to think it was because I was
taller than a lot of the other girls, but then I would see other tall girls making perfect turns. It was something that I just
couldn't change—kind of like the fact that I only used a two-
beat kick. I was one of the only swimmers out there doing that.
It wasn't that I didn't want to try a four or six-beat kick. I just
wasn't coordinated enough to do it. A six-beat kick would make
me feel as if I were swimming way too slow. I just could not get
used to it.

One day at practice, Mark asked me about it.

"Have you always swam like that?" he said.

I explained it all to him and even demonstrated what happened when I tried to alter my kick. He laughed, shrugged his
shoulders, and said, "It's okay. You're fine just the way you are.
Don't worry about it. Focus on your strengths."

That was Mark. Always focusing on the positive. As I was
wrapping up a lane after a good practice, he would always kneel
down and say just say one word of encouragement to me, like
"superior" or "superb" or "wonderful." That always meant a lot
to me. It always pushed me to do a little better. But he was
strict, too. If you were not at practice on time, you were not

allowed in. He'd actually close the gate and lock it! Everybody knew that, so it was rare for anyone to show up late.

Mark's practices were always fun and never boring. He was creative and innovative. Like Flip, he became a very positive male role model. Flip had always told me that swimming was like having a bank account: the more you put in, the more you got out of it. I believed in his philosophy, and I tried to step it up even more when I was at practice with him.

Every day, Mark made all of his swimmers fill out a logbook of their progress. He wanted us to record what our best times had been, how we felt about those times, and what we felt we needed to do to improve. I wasn't too crazy about this. I was very intense and focused on my swimming, and didn't think I needed any device like a journal to help me swim stronger. I also didn't have time for it; practicing that many hours a day and going to school full-time left essentially zero free time, and the last thing I wanted to do was answer a bunch of questions. I was becoming more and more strong-willed, and I finally told him at one point that I wasn't going to fill out the book. He didn't fight me on it. I think he respected me and understood how hard I was working. If he had really felt that a journal would've helped me, I'm sure he would have pushed for it.

Right after we swam the Nationals, Mark would sit down alone with each of us and talk about where we needed to be in the next year. This was one of the things he did that I loved the most. He would throw out absolutely insane times that he thought you were capable of swimming. Most of us would share stories later about the numbers he had given us, and we would shake our heads at how unrealistic they were. We just couldn't swim that fast.

But then the next year would roll around and—lo and behold!—we would get those times that he had given us. That's the kind of genius Mark was. He always had a plan in his head for you, and as ambitious as it would seem, he knew what you had in you and that he could help get you there. After you made the time, he'd pull you aside and whisper, "See, I told you that you could do it. Keep working hard and you can do whatever you set your mind to."

In our first year back from Munich, a law was passed called Title IX, which required gender equality for boys and girls in every educational program that received federal funding. All of the sudden, I was allowed to swim on a boys' team—and I did. More often than not, I beat the boys on the Fountain Valley High School boys' team. I squeezed school meets in-between my late practices, which made for an even crazier schedule. But those meets helped push me and make me stronger. Even though the Olympics were still three years off, everything I did was in preparation for the Games.

CHAPTER SEVEN

What Happened to the East Germans?

Things started getting exciting for me in 1973. People were asking to meet me when I swam. In February of that year, at a local meet in East Los Angeles called the First Annual World Invitational Swim Meet, Kirk Douglas told my mom that he wanted to meet me. He was lovely and complimentary when he shook my hand on the pool deck.

"Shirley, I'm a big fan of yours," he said. "My family has been following you since the Olympics last year, and we're all really excited to follow your career. We'll be rooting for you all the way."

That spring, our team spent the day at Disneyland with some other swimmers, and who was there but Shane Gould. She had moved to Northern California from Australia for the time being to attend high school there. We chatted for a little while and had our photo taken together in front of the Magic Castle.

In April, after the Nationals, I headed back to Europe and swam at the gorgeous Crystal Palace in London for an international invitational meet. My old team, Phillips 66, helped sponsor our travel and I got to see older traditional English tourist spots, from Big Ben to Buckingham Palace. But the most memorable part of trip was more personal—it was on this trip that I had my first real kiss.

Our team was staying in a British youth hostel and one night, a swimmer I had met named Kurt Krumpholz invited me to his room. He was a couple of years older than me, but he was really cute. That night, alone in his room, with my stomach full of butterflies, he leaned over and kissed me. That's all that happened. I didn't really know what to do, but I knew that I loved the feeling. Between all the practices and competitions, I didn't get a lot of chances to really experience being a teenager. This was my moment.

Eventually, when we returned to California, Kurt showed up at my house and asked if he could take me on a date. I met him at the door and told him in an urgent and hushed tone that he had to leave. He wasn't Russian, and for that I think my mother would've killed me. So much for getting to be a teenager.

There were other trips that stood out as well—the U.S. Nationals in Cincinnati in April, along with several other competitions. But that year, everything was leading up to the FINA World Aquatics Championships in late August, which would be held in Belgrade, Yugoslavia.

I was so excited to be going to Belgrade. In that first year working with Mark, I felt as if I'd grown much stronger as a swimmer. He was a much more intense coach than Flip had been, and his workouts had already had a huge impact on my abilities. After the '72 Olympics, I was very conscious of how I would present myself to the world on major stages like that. For me, the '76 Games were going to be a bit of a coming out party. I'd done well at the '72 Olympics, but now I wanted to dazzle everybody and really prove that I belonged.

The first FINA Championships, held at the Tasmajdan Sports Centre in Belgrade, would include competitions in swimming, diving, high diving, synchronized swimming, and water polo. It was a very big deal, almost like a mini-Olympics, featuring athletes from all over the world.

We flew into Belgrade on August 29. The next day, we headed over to the pool so we could get a feel for the place and hold a practice before the competition. Getting used to the pool was always important.

We suited up at the hotel and then hopped on the bus and made our way over to the complex. Belgrade struck me as very European; it was old and had a cultured look. To me, it lacked the color of West Germany and felt more stark and monochromatic, like East Germany. Then again, when you're born and raised in sunny California, many places tend to look a little drab.

Our bus pulled up outside the complex, which, like many European pools, felt very old and even sort of Gothic. Excited, we hopped off the bus and made our way up the steps to the main doorway. But when we tried to open the doors, we discovered that they were locked.

"There must be a mistake," one of our coaches said. "Let me see if I can find another way in."

We stood on the street together, chattering and gawking at the buildings while we waited. A few minutes later, our coach returned looking puzzled.

"That's weird," he said. "All the doors are locked."

By that time, another coach had wandered off to find out what was going on, since we had arrived at our appointed time. He came back with a curious look on his face.

"Well," he said, "I found somebody at the side gate who told me we aren't allowed in right now."

We all asked him why not, and he shrugged his shoulders.

"They told me we aren't allowed in there because the East

Germans aren't finished practicing yet."

"That's pretty ridiculous," I said. "How come they get the whole place to themselves?"

"That's a good question," he said. "I don't know."

None of us had ever heard of anything like this happening before. No team ever got to have an entire facility all to itself. If your team arrived early, you would just sit on the deck and wait until the other team cleared out. No big deal. We had never been locked out while another team practiced.

We stood outside for about ten minutes, wondering what to do. Finally, we heard the locks turning in the main entrance. A swimming official opened the doors and motioned for us to come inside, like the coast was clear. What was going on?

We made our way through the cavernous building to the outdoor pool, which was beautiful. There was not one trace of the East German team anywhere. Not a single soul. It was very strange. Wow, I thought, it's almost as if they're being hidden from us. But I didn't want to get psyched out by my competition. I was in Belgrade to prove that I was ready for the next level, and once I dove in to run a few practice laps, all I could think about was competing the next day.

One person I wouldn't be swimming against at this meet was Shane Gould. Incredibly, she had retired earlier that summer at just seventeen years old—only about a year older than me. The media pressure had become too much for her. I remember thinking that the press could have given her a little more space after learning why she retired. She was such an amazing swimmer. She is the only person, male or female, to hold every world freestyle record from 100 meters to 1,500 meters and the 200-meter individual medley world record simultaneously, which she did from December 1971 to September 1972. She was the first female swimmer ever to win three Olympic gold medals in world record time, and the first swimmer, male or female, to win Olympic medals in five individual events in a single Olympics. Very impressive. I was almost sorry that she wasn't going to be there anymore; swimmers of her caliber really pushed you to do your best.

We did our warm-ups, then called it a day and went back to the hotel to get a good night's rest.

When we got to the pool the next morning, the energy at the facility was very different. Thousands of fans were starting to gather, and all of the teams had arrived—from Great Britain, France, Sweden, Hungary, Australia, Russia, and Japan, among others. Interestingly, we still didn't see the East German team.

We went to the locker room to get changed and then gathered together on the deck as the race times grew closer. There was a buzz in the air, with lots of electricity from all the excited fans. This competition really felt like a big deal.

Then something caught my eye. Silently and stoically, the East German female swimmers paraded out of the locker room in a single file line. At least, I thought they were the East German female swimmers. Like I said, I hadn't paid much attention to them at the '72 Olympics because they simply weren't that good or memorable. But I did remember that they all had looked . . . well, like women. What I saw filing out of the locker room was quite unusual.

Many of the same girls I had seen the year before were there, but their physical characteristics had changed. They were all very muscular, but not the kind of muscular you get from working out. It was if their body types had changed. Their shoulders were broader, and they were walking differently. At a half glance, I would have thought it was the male team coming out.

"Hey," I said to my friend, Kathy Heddy, "do they look weird to you?"

"Yeah," Kathy replied. "They seem bigger or something."

I couldn't quite put my finger on it, but something seemed

wrong with them. They didn't look at any of the other teams, and they didn't speak to anybody. They just filed past, almost like robots, and gathered on their own side of the pool. Their coaches kept a tight circle around them, as if they didn't want them socializing with anybody on any level.

Now, I understand that race day isn't the best time to go out and make new friends around the pool. But in the spirit of competition and sportsmanship, we would often acknowledge our competitors and exchange pleasantries. Like us, most of them were young people who were also traveling the world and representing their country. So we had that in common. It was fun to share a quick exchange with each other, maybe about your experiences abroad so far. There was nothing wrong with that. In fact, it often helped ease a lot of the pressure on race day. But the East Germans were having none of it. They were in their own world.

Once the competition began, it became obvious that something radical had happened to the East German team since the year before. They had become phenomenal. They were killing us from the outset. It was ridiculous. To improve that much in one year was astounding. I had more than doubled the mileage I was swimming at home, and I felt incredibly strong. I had been looking forward to showing off my strength. But it paled in comparison to what the East Germans brought. They looked much bigger and stronger, and when they swam, it looked effortless. At the end of each race, they weren't even winded. They would touch the wall at the end and literally hop out of the pool.

It was obvious to me that something was up. But, being only sixteen years old, I didn't know much about drug use or steroids. None of my teammates did, either. When I asked a friend of mine if she had ever seen anything like this before, she just stared ahead, wide-eyed and silent, and shook her head.

At the '72 Games in Munich, the East German team had occupied twelve places in the finals and won two silvers and a bronze. But at the FINA Championships in Belgrade, just one year later, they won ten of the fourteen gold medals, as well as five silvers and three bronzes. They had five 1–2 finishes. They also set *nine* world records.

I couldn't believe how badly the East Germans had beaten us; it was like swimming against aliens. We'd trounced them just a year before. Our team was in shock—how had we gotten killed like that? Except for my teammate Melissa Belote's silver and gold in the backstroke races, not one American won a medal better than a bronze in a non-freestyle individual event. I came away with four silver medals, and all but one of them were behind East German swimmers. Kornelia Ender won four golds and a silver. Ulrike Richter, Renate Vogel, and Andrea Hübner also turned heads with their performances.

The East German team suddenly seemed to be shrouded in mystery. We never heard them speak anymore. We never saw them practice. They became like shadows, coming and going quietly. To many observers, the veil that shrouded them was exotic; it gave them mystique and hinted at some sort of "super program" that had to be protected for fear of other countries stealing their precious secrets. Swimming was growing more and more popular, and with heavy promotion on TV programs like *ABC's Wide World of Sports*, the East German team was getting more coverage than ever. All of the sudden, a small and depressed country was showcasing the best swimmers in the world.

This phenomenon was explained away with the East Germans' new "skinsuits," which were said to be remarkably efficient in the water. The suits may have helped a little bit, but my teammates and I knew that they weren't the only factor.

When I returned home, the new issue of *Swimming World* contained what I found to be a blockbuster story.

It began:

WHY ARE THESE GERMANS SO GOOD?

It seems every year a new swim star emerges and dominates in the sport. Great names like Schollander, Spitz, and Gould come to mind, but 1973 is destined to be the their year. The season is still young, with the major championships to come, and this young 15-year-old East German sensation has bettered two world records and three European marks. Her pending world records include the 100 fly in 103.05 and the 200 IM in 223.01. Besides these two events, her third European record is the 100 free in 58.6.1. At age 13, she won the European junior title in the 200 IM, and was the youngest winner at that meet. Since then, her progress has been steady and relentless. Ender will lead the East German girls' team in Belgrade in September, and should emerge as one of the luminaries of that championship.

Okay, I got it. Everyone was fascinated now by the leaps and bounds that Kornelia Ender had made. But then the article reprinted a piece by French journalist Jean-Pierre Lacour:

For a long time, everyone's curiosity has been aroused by the success of the East German swimmers, especially as they jealously keep the secrets of their success to themselves. It is extremely difficult to talk to any team member from East Germany without the presence of some official being always present. They have refused access to their training centers to both foreign and East German journalists. Thanks to a coach from one of the Eastern countries, who for obvious reasons wishes to remain anonymous, a little bit of the mystery may be uncovered. The coach in question has spent considerable time with and also took part in the East German training program.

His statements can be substantiated by simply observing that the appearance of the East German swimmers were considerably changed from a year ago. Also, many coaches from other countries have similar opinions about the reasons behind East Germany's successes.

The annual training plan is divided into three phases—endurance, speed endurance, and speed. Eight days of rest separate each phase.

The daily training distance is about 10 km, 340 days per year. The doctors make sure that all the training is never allowed to exceed the limits of each athlete. This is done mainly by frequent blood tests. There is talk of a sort of "vaccine" against fatigue. It consists of an injection of toxic substances, which allows the body to combat fatigue more efficiently. It is believed that male hormones are given to the girls, who, in addition to an increase in vigor, develop a superiority complex with respect to other females from foreign countries. Another device is the use of a doping substance, not currently detectable, which virtually guarantees maximum performance with 98% chance of success, as compared to classic training, which is about 68% successful. These accusations are terrible. The only way for East German to distance themselves from these accusations is to open their training camps. A simple denial will not be sufficient.

I kept reading over those words: "There is talk of a sort of 'vaccine' against fatigue." Vaccine? Why hadn't this *Swimming World* piece rocked the swimming world? I showed the article to other swimmers at practice, but everyone just shrugged it off.

Mark told me that they were rumors and they might be true, but until proven otherwise, we just had to keep swimming harder.

This needs to be looked into, I thought to myself. But it never happened. The article came and went without a whisper.

CHAPTER EIGHT

Skinsuits and
a Mysterious Vaccine

In the wake of the drubbing we took in Belgrade, Mark continued to work us hard back home at practice. He would throw us in the animal lane, which was basically the lane where the strongest swimmers practiced every day. I was the only girl in the animal lane, swimming hard against the boys. Mark really loved watching me kill the guys in that lane, especially when I broke world records doing laps. I loved it, too.

Although I missed Flip, Mark's youthfulness and energy was refreshing. We swimmers could relate to him because he felt more like one of us. He was still the boss and our coach, but he was cool. He was close enough to us in age that we really trusted him.

After Belgrade, Mark made sure that we all started swimming in the skinsuits that had been all the rage at the competition. I will admit that they felt very different from our regular swimsuits. It was almost like swimming naked. In fact, *Sports Illustrated* ran a photo of me wearing a black one, and I looked practically naked. The suits weighed a mere two ounces and were made of paper-thin Lycra that revealed pretty much everything, down to any goosebumps you might have had. At one meet, a photographer was taking pictures of a group of female swimmers in the skintight suits, and Donna de Varona asked him, "Don't you feel like a dirty old man?"

After the East Germans' performance at Belgrade, everyone started thinking it was all about the suits. But I was skeptical.

"I know the suits are better," I said to Mark one day at practice, "but it doesn't explain what I saw in Belgrade. Those girls weren't just swimming differently. They were behaving differently. They never got tired, and they swam like robots. There's no bathing suit in the world that can change how you swim."

Throughout 1974, I juggled my senior year of high school with a lot of travel to swim in competitions. In February, I competed in the International Invitational in France. I swam the 100, the 200, and the 800 free, and I did pretty well. I just loved Paris. I was excited to visit because I had taken so many years of French in school, and this was my chance to try it out.

A couple of weeks later, we headed back home for the 1974 Southern California Invitational. Then, in April, I flew to Dallas for the AAU Short Course Championships. It was the first major swim meet where skirts were not required on women's suits. But I wasn't thinking that much about the bathing suits; I was focused on the races. At that meet, I set two individual American records, one in the 200 free and another in the 500 free. I also set two American records and relays: the 400 free relay and the 800 free relay.

Wherever I swam, people were talking about the Montreal Olympics coming up in two years. Whispers were turning into outright predictions. "Will Shirley Babashoff be the one to beat in '76?" "Will Shirley Babashoff be America's next Mark Spitz?" It was starting to get crazy, and we still had two years to go until the Games.

In May 1974, I swam in the Mount San Antonio Senior Meet in Walnut, California, and won the 100, 200, 400, and

1,500 freestyle events and the 200 and 400 individual medley events. Afterwards, my friend Kathy Heddy said to me, "You know that everyone gets scared when you walk out on the deck, right? You know that you get in people's heads just by showing up, right?"

I laughed. I knew what she was talking about, and I liked it. As a competitor, you want to be the one who intimidates everyone. At least, I wanted to. If I got into their heads, then I had a huge advantage before I even got in the water. At that point, it was getting easy to a point of almost boredom for me at meets. Since I swam on boys' teams in high school (and would soon do the same in college) and only practiced against boys in the animal lane where Mark put his strongest swimmers, swimming against women was becoming too easy. That is, except for the East Germans.

Next was the Santa Clara Invitational, and then in August, the Los Angeles Invitational, where I won the 100 free, the 200 free, and the 400 free. There was no rest for the weary; after each competition, I would head home for a couple of weeks and swim my usual twenty miles a day at practice, and then it would start all over again when I traveled to the next event. But I was really enjoying myself. The trips were like bonuses you received after working so hard in the pool. I had caught the travel bug on that first trip to Europe; though I was working hard to win meets, I also knew that the more I won, the more I would be able to tour the world.

In August, I headed up to the 1974 Long Course Nationals in Concord, California. This competition would set the table for our "dual meet" a week later with the East Germans, which was breathlessly anticipated by the media.

Concord was charming and quaint, like a real-life Mayberry from *The Andy Griffith Show*. There was something about the pool at Concord Community Park that just felt right. I'd competed there before and had really liked it.

A few days before the Nationals started, we heard that in Vienna, Austria, East Germany's Kornelia Ender had set a world record in the 200-meter freestyle, swimming a time of 2:03.22. Clearly, she was getting better every day. But at the Nationals, battling against my friend Kim Peyton, I was able to shatter Ender's record with a world record time of 2:02.94. That felt good, kind of like I was sending a message back to Austria.

For the Nationals, all the winners and second-place finishers would form the U.S. national swimming team, which would then square off against East Germans. We had a week to kill until they arrived, so we all stayed in Concord and had a chance to relax mentally and physically.

There was a lot of talk about the East Germans, and a lot of concern about what had happened a year earlier in Belgrade. One day, I was hanging around the pool after a light practice with my friend, John Naber, and we were talking about the East German team.

"It's really weird what's happening with those girls," I said. "I don't think it's the same on the guy's side, but I still can't understand how the women's team is getting so strong. It just doesn't make any sense."

John agreed, but neither of us had any real answers. There was definitely a heightened interest in the upcoming dual meet, since it would pit us against the newly revitalized East German team. That was becoming a regular storyline in the media— the East Germans were viewed as the underdogs, the upstarts, the Davids who were looking to upset the Goliaths. Everybody loves a story like that. But, of course, it's a much better story if the Davids are not acting secretive and suspicious.

My old coach, Flip, was at the Nationals, too, as part of our coaching staff. While he had stopped coaching teams on a regular basis, he still took part in certain major events. One day after practice, he and I reminisced about the '72 Games.

"It's interesting, isn't it," he said. "Back then, we hardly paid any attention to the East German girls. Whoever thought that, after the Games, they'd be this kind of powerhouse all of the sudden? I can hardly even remember them from Munich."

I nodded. "It's not really possible to get that good that fast, is it?" I asked him.

"I don't know what to tell you," he replied. "I'll admit that I've never seen anything like it. But their government is evidently very involved in their program. They're obviously committing a lot of resources to it, so maybe they've just figured out a better way to train. They seem to pass the drug tests everyone has to take, so what else could it be?"

I was curious to see exactly what the East Germans would look like by now. The shock we had felt when we'd seen them in Belgrade still hadn't worn off. When we arrived at the pool to practice for the next day's races against the East Germans, I looked around for them. But they weren't there.

"Are the East Germans here yet?" I asked our coach, Jack Nelson.

"They came and they left," he replied. "I heard that they got here early when nobody was here, and then they left quietly after that. Nobody even saw them."

In other words, it sounded like business as usual from the East Germans.

The next day, they finally appeared. I watched them walk out onto the deck, stoic and robotic as ever. They walked past us without making any eye contact or saying a word, just as they had in Belgrade. They looked even bigger and more muscular than they had the year before, almost like weightlifters.

Swimmers never looked like that. This wasn't just about the sk-insuits.

The reporters at the competition kept asking me how I felt I was going to do against Ender in the 200 free, given the numbers we had both posted within the last couple of weeks.

"I'm here to win," I said. "I don't care as much about the numbers as I do about beating the competition, and that's what my plan is."

Suffice it to say, I think a lot of people were disappointed when Ender scratched from the 200 free, claiming that she was under the weather. I thought that was really strange. The East Germans were fiercely competitive; it was hard to imagine any of them pulling out of a race.

Ender's absence didn't stop me from unleashing another 2:02.94, matching my record time from a week earlier. I also won the 400, took a silver in the 800, and anchored the 400 free relay with my friends, Kathy Heddy, Ann Marshall, and Kim Peyton. We set a world record in that event. Ender's illness notwithstanding, the East German women swam remarkably well. They were certainly a team to contend with, and we were fighting for our pride. But we beat them 198–145, a far cry from the 98–66 drubbing we had endured in Belgrade.

The biggest story that came out of that dual meet, though, was from the men's competition. My dear friend John Naber had defeated the legendary East German Roland Matthes in the 200-meter backstroke. It was the first time he had lost that race since 1967 (John also beat him in the 100). It was an absolutely awesome performance by John and instantly became the highlight of the competition. Our other guys did well, too—Steve Furniss achieved a world record in the 200 individual medley, and John Hencken set world records in both breast-stroke events.

CHAPTER NINE

Swimming with the College Boys

By the end of the Long Course Nationals, it was clear: the East Germans were not going away, and we needed to deal with it. Whatever was going on, they were getting bigger and stronger. As I thought ahead to the 1976 Olympics, I began to realize that my swimming career was now basically on a crash collision course against the East Germans. There was no way around it. No matter how hard I trained, I knew that they were going to be bigger and badder.

After Concord, whenever I tried to talk about the East Germans' remarkable—and unbelievable—strength, I was brushed off.

"They're just working really hard, Shirley," my teammates and coaches told me. "That's what we have to do—work harder."

I didn't mind working hard. What I did mind was that the East German female team was improving at a rate that seemed bizarre and unnatural. I knew what it took to be a strong swimmer, and there was no way that one or two years could produce what they were doing. No way at all. I could not forget about the East Germans' "vaccine" that I had read about in *Swimming World*. It was stuck in my brain.

Just as our coaches had switched our team over to skinsuits to keep up with the East Germans, they were now talking about adding weights to our regimen and focusing more on building our physiques. That's how influential the East Germans had become—they were in everyone's head, even Coach Mark's. After learning that the East Germans conducted regular blood tests to rest the girls whose white blood cell counts were high due to possible infection, he decided to do the same thing with our team. It was all about staying even with the new leaders, the East Germans.

I told Mark there was no way I was going to agree to blood tests. Nobody was going to pull me out of the water, even if I was a little sick. I swam no matter what. But plenty of other kids on our team were getting tested. In Mission Viejo, a little table was set up by the pool where kids stopped to get their blood drawn after practice. If anyone showed even a trace of infection, they were not allowed to swim the next day.

I wasn't convinced that skinsuits and blood tests were the only factors in the East Germans' success.

"I almost feel crazy," I said to my friend, Kelly Hamill, after practice one day. "Like I'm the only one who sees what is going on."

"You're not crazy," she said. "But maybe they just can't do anything about it."

But I was getting better, too. My trick? Wearing a t-shirt in the water to create drag, so I had to swim harder. When I arrived at a competition, all of the other swimmers stopped what they were doing to look at me. I was becoming the one to beat. Every day, I became a little bit more competitive, and I suppose with that came a bit of arrogance. I could be abrupt with people. I would even play a few head games before a race, by simply standing next to my opponents and staring down at them. Intimidation definitely plays a part in competition, and I had no problem letting everybody else know that I was there to win.

One of the highlights of my year was being invited to take part in something called the Gillette Cavalcade of Champions, hosted by Bob Hope at the Century Plaza Hotel in Los Angeles. It was an awards show and variety show blended into one, and showcased some of the best athletes in the world. I posed for photos with Muhammad Ali, Jack Nicklaus, Billie Jean King, Steve Garvey, Julius Erving, and many others. It really shows just how popular swimming was at that time, for me to have been included with all of those legends. I was pretty nervous and didn't say too much to any of them, but they were all very nice to me.

Ali was especially sweet. "You gonna teach me how to swim, little girl?" he asked, wide-eyed and smiling. I really liked him.

After graduating from Fountain Valley High School in 1974, I enrolled at the nearby Golden West College in Huntington Beach with hopes of getting a degree in marine biology one day. Of course, I was going to swim there, too. I really liked the college's coach, Tom Hermstad. When we first met, I asked him if I could try out for the men's team.

"Hey, you can do whatever you like," he replied. "If you can compete with the boys, we are happy to have you."

Tom was a great coach to work with. I squeezed college meets in between my practices at Mission Viejo and other competitions, and Tom coordinated with Mark to make my practice schedule something that would work for everyone. "Herm," as we called him, was totally supportive of me. When some of the guys on his team acted a little upset that they suddenly had a girl to compete with, Herm let them know in no uncertain terms that I was a part of the squad and that if they had any issues with me, they could beat me in the pool.

I juggled my trips, classes, practices, and meets as best I could and had almost zero time for any kind of social life. For me, all roads were leading to the '76 Games, and I wasn't going to let anything stop me.

Wrapping up 1974, *Swimming World* named me the "Female American Swimmer of the Year." That felt really good and was a great start to 1975. In January, I was featured on the cover of *Aquatic World* magazine. In the interview, the subject of the East Germans' strength came up. Although my suspicions were swirling in my head, I wasn't quite ready to share them in print:

> AQUATIC WORLD: *How did [the World Championships in Belgrade] compare with the Olympics?*

> SHIRLEY BABASHOFF: *Well, the East Germans were a lot better. And a lot of our swimmers were kind of down about how big the East Germans were and how well they were doing. So we didn't really have the psychological advantage there—especially when they beat us in the first event 4–100-meter relay. Right after that, everybody on our team was really down.*

> AW: *How did you do in that meet?*

> SB: *I got four seconds—two in the relays, one in the 100-meter free, and another one in the 200-meter free.*

> AW: *How did you feel about getting the seconds? Were you disappointed?*

> SB: *Well I'd rather be first, you know, but it's better than getting third.*

> AW: *You've swum against the East Germans for a number of years—first when they weren't very strong internationally and now when they are very strong indeed. What are your impressions of how they've developed?*

> SB: *Well, we weren't expecting it. That's another reason we*

didn't do that well at the World Games. It just popped up. And it was kind of a shock, really. But you have to try to prepare for that kind of thing.

AW: *How do you think the much-publicized skinsuit helped the East Germans at the World Championships? Do you feel that made a big difference?*

SB: *Well, the suit certainly helps you. When we saw the suit at the World Championships that was another thing against us—because it makes your shoulders look bigger, and the East Germans were big already. They were tall, kind of built like boys, I guess you'd say—maybe they do a lot of weights or something. But all of that kind of went along with it. We thought, this is a wonder suit and we're never going to keep them from beating us and everybody was just super down. But later on we got the suit. We swam against them last August, court and we did really well. But see, there we were prepared for it.*

Throughout 1975, my schedule was more of the same. Twenty miles every day, sandwiched between school classes and travel to various competitions and exhibitions. Swimming had become like a full-time job, but I was still focused on getting good grades at school, so I worked extra hard.

My practices under Mark were clearly paying off. I was becoming almost unbeatable. In March, I swam in the Southern California Invitational at East Los Angeles College. I won the 100, 200, and 500 free, came second in the 200 individual medley, and third in the 400 individual medley. In April, I went to the AAU Short Course Swimming National Championships at the Keating Natatorium in Cincinnati, where I won the 100,

200, and 500 free and came in third in the 400 individual medley.

The following month, I swam at the Western Olympic Development Meet in Long Beach and won the 100, 200, 400, and
800 free, along with the 200 and 400 individual medley. At the
World Swimming Championship Trials in June, I won the 100
and 200 free while setting a world record and an American record in the 400 free. I also placed second in the 800 free and the
200 individual medley.

One of the trips I took over the summer was to Monaco, along France's Mediterranean coastline. A group of other
American swimmers and I were there to perform a swimming
exhibition for some of the citizens and local dignitaries.

Monaco was an absolutely stunning place, unlike anything
I'd ever seen before. It was just so elegant and picturesque. On
one of our afternoons off, we all headed to the beach for a refreshing dip in the beautiful blue waters of the Mediterranean.
Somehow, Prince Albert heard that we were in town, and he
decided to join us. Frolicking out in the sea with him, he just
seemed like a normal teenager. I didn't even think about the
fact that he was royalty, or that his mom was Grace Kelly. He
was just a cute guy taking a swim with the rest of us, and he was
really good company. He and I were about the same age at the
time. He was a pretty good swimmer.

"I love how you swim," he said to me. "You make it look so
easy."

Later that night, after we swam in our exhibition, there was
a ceremony that Prince Albert presided over. He was presenting
me with an award, and after I accepted it, he leaned over and
gave me a kiss on the cheek. I couldn't believe it. Getting kissed
by a prince. Sometimes, those eight hours of practice every day
really paid off.

We flew back to the United States for the Nationals, which

would be held at the Belmont Plaza Pool in Long Beach. The historic indoor pool had become like a home away from home for me. I'd had many meets there, and it was a very comfortable venue for me. Plus, it was only about twenty minutes from my house. I swam well there, beating my own world record in the 400-meter freestyle with a 4:14.76 time, knocking more than a second off the world record mark I'd set in Concord back in 1974 at the dual meet versus East Germany. Overall, I qualified in both the 400-meter and 200-meter freestyles, as well as the 200-meter individual medley to represent our country in Cali, Colombia. I was also happy for my pal Kathy Heddy, who came in second behind me in the 400 at 4:15.57, which was also faster than my previous record in Concord. After the 400, Kathy and I hugged on the pool deck, excited at the thought of another big trip in just a couple of weeks.

Our training camp to prepare for the championships in Colombia was at the same pool in Buena Park where, as a nine-year-old, I'd been a member of the Splashers. I felt strange and kind of nostalgic being back in that same pool at William Peak Park. So much had changed for me since then. I showed off my old stomping grounds to my teammates and Flip, who would be leading the team again.

We trained hard, but we still had fun. One night, our coaches piled us all into a van to go to the drive-in and see the big movie of the summer, *Jaws*. In my mind, that big shark was a kind of metaphor for the East German team: silent, predatory, and quite dangerous.

A few days later, we boarded our charter flight for Colombia. When we arrived, it seemed like every reporter we came across wanted to talk about the East Germans.

"How do you think you'll do against the East Germans, Shirley?"

"Are you nervous about facing the East Germans?"

"How tough do you think the East Germans will be next year at the Olympics?"

Wherever I went, the media asked more and more about the East Germans. It was as if the East Germans were the only competitors I had on the planet now.

We took a couple of days to settle in and enjoy Cali. We heard that silver was super inexpensive there, so we went shopping for anything made of silver. I bought a beautiful bracelet; I still have it. Flip also told me about a place that gave manicures for three dollars, so the other girls and I headed there and got our nails painted red, white, and blue.

After we had settled in and seen the sights, we went to Unidad Deportiva Panamericana, the swimming complex where the championships would be held. We held practice to get used to the water and check everything out, and as usual, the East Germans were nowhere to be seen. Their pattern was set. They moved in and out like phantoms, quiet and nearly invisible. The championships featured 682 aquatic athletes from 39 different nations, and it was good to see some of the acquaintances I had made over the years. Like Belgrade, it was a mini-Olympics kind of environment.

On July 19, the day of the opening ceremonies and first events, we finally got a glimpse of the mysterious East Germans. Even in their warm-up gear, I could tell that they had gotten bigger and broader. They were even scarier than they had been in Concord.

I nudged my friend Kathy. "Look at them," I said. "You think that's normal?"

She shook her head, staring at the muscular team. But nobody said anything—not a word from the coaches or anyone else. It was as if everyone was too polite to comment.

Once the races started, it was obvious that the East Germans had gotten even stronger. But I'd been working hard, too, and I performed better in the competition than I had in Concord the year before. I won a gold medal in the 200-meter freestyle, defeating my new archnemesis Kornelia Ender with a time of 2:02.50 to set a meet *and* an American record. Earlier that day, Ender had set the previous meet record in the event with a 2:04.07 time in the qualifying round. I also won gold in the 400-meter freestyle. However, the silver medals in the 100 freestyle and the relay events fell into the hands of the East Germans. This was becoming a regular pattern: my silver to East German gold. In the 100 freestyle, I won a bronze medal.

My six-medal haul seemed to set me up for the Olympics the next year. I was excited, feeding off the buzz in Colombia about the Montreal Games. The media began hyping the Shirley-Babashoff-versus-the-East-Germans story even more. To the rest of the world, the East Germans made for a sensational story. They were young, disciplined, and focused. The media had given the East Germans cute little nicknames, like "the Flying Frauleins" and "the Wundermachen" ("Wonder Machine"). But in Cali, on the rare occasions when I was close enough to hear Kornelia Ender and her teammates speak, their baritone voices were hardly cute. Each time I saw them, upon closer inspection, they were becoming more and more like men—their physiques, voices, and especially how they swam.

"I'm glad I swim on the Golden West College men's team," I whispered to Kathy one day before a race. "They've prepared me for this."

No world records were broken in Cali, but Kathy made big news when she won the 200-meter individual medley by beating East German Ulrike Tauber, catching her in the final five meters after trailing the entire race. It was thrilling, and I was so proud of her.

Coming home from Cali, any idea that the East Germans were going away had been completely erased. True, they didn't blow us out. We swam well. But they were definitely the team to look out for, without even a close second. They won more gold medals than we did in Cali—ten to our three—but our team won the overall tournament. The Associated Press ran this piece, which summed it up:

> The tears that flowed at Belgrade haven't turned into a flood of gold medals for the American women swimmers yet, but there is still another year until the Montreal Olympics. Swimming programs can turn as quickly as a freestyler switches from one lap to the next. At the 1972 Olympics, East Germany didn't create any waves when its men's backstroker, Roland Matthes, claimed the tiny country's only two gold medals. Then came Belgrade, and the shock of East German female supremacy in the pool that hit the Americans with the force of a belly flop off the high tower.

That was true. But the East Germans had failed to blow us out in Cali, which no doubt sent a message to the small country. I wondered how they would retaliate in Montreal.

The media kept talking about Kornelia Ender and me in the same breath. One reporter stopped me in the hotel lobby and said, "Shirley, next year's going to be remarkable watching you and Ender compete in Montreal." As if it were going to be a two-person Olympics.

Getting on the plane back to California, Flip said to me, "Shirley, you swam beautifully. You know they're going to be tough next summer. You see how they improve each year. But you're getting stronger, too. They know it. They're watching you closely. They know you can beat them."

CHAPTER TEN

My Personal Best

My best friends on the road were Kathy Heddy and Camille Wright. We were all about the same age, and they were both adventurous and made me laugh so much. When we traveled, it seemed like the older swimmers never liked to go out. Even though they were in their twenties, some of them acted like they were in their fifties. We teenage girls, on the other hand, were always up for anything. We would sometimes get into a little trouble, but nothing too terrible; it was usually something along the lines of getting lost in the city or trying to sneak a beer here and there. They made every trip an adventure, and I relied on their friendship.

They were both great swimmers, too. Camille won three gold medals at the 1975 Pan American Games in Mexico City, including the 100-meter and 200-meter butterfly events, and was a member of the winning U.S. team in the 4×100-meter medley relay. At the World Aquatics Championships in Cali, she received a silver medal as a member of the second-place U.S. team in the 4×100-meter medley relay, and a bronze in the 100-meter butterfly. Kathy was also a very strong swimmer, and made the Olympic team with me in 1976.

After we returned from Cali, I swam in the Mission Viejo Invitational and won the 100 free and 200 individual medley.

Later that summer, I competed in the AAU National Long Course Championships in Kansas City and also did very well, winning the 100, 200, and 400 free and coming in fourth in the 200 individual medley. In August, I flew to Tokyo for the Japanese National Championships, where I won the 100, 200, and 400 free while taking third in the 200 individual medley.

For all the traveling I had done, there was nothing like the peace and tranquility of Japan. The gardens were so beautiful and perfect. I remember thinking, what a perfect place to meditate. But the cities like Tokyo and Kyoto were the exact opposite, brighter and crazier than the Las Vegas Strip.

We also squeezed in a trip to Tunisia, where we participated in an exhibition, and got to visit Morocco as well. One pool we swam in seemed like it was filled with ocean water. It was right on the beach and it had seaweed in it and some fish, too, so we wore our goggles. At one point, Kathy's goggles fell off and we started laughing—but the Tunisian swimmers thought we are laughing at them. The next day, the local newspapers accused us of being ugly Americans, which really hurt because it was nothing of the sort. They called us "disrespectful" and "arrogant." Still, we were so good that we were getting a reputation around the world as being a little full of ourselves.

In the fall of 1975, I was voted Homecoming Queen at Golden West College. I was happy to do something that wasn't swimming-related and get to dress up and be girly for a change. A couple of months later, my coach, Mark, made Christmas very special for us by taking a group from the Nadadores swimming team to Hawaii. We participated in a small exhibition there, but Mark made sure that the trip was more like a vacation for us, since we had been practicing so hard for the past couple of years.

Another good friend of mine, Kelly Hamill, was on the trip, too. Because she lived in Fountain Valley, we always drove to practice together in Mission Viejo. One day on our Hawaii trip, a few of us, including Brian Goodell and Kelly, went down to the beach at high tide and found a giant rock with waves crashing against it. We decided to take a picture on the rock, but we misjudged the high tide; a huge wave knocked us off the rock and sucked me out into the ocean. Everybody else was able to scramble back to shore pretty easily, but in just a minute or two I found myself about 300 yards offshore and struggling. I was a strong swimmer, but I felt so out of control out in the ocean, caught in a riptide. I forced myself to relax and reminded myself that I was only about twelve pool lengths from the shore. That was nothing. I paced myself and made it back to shore.

We came home from Hawaii and all of the sudden, it was 1976. It was the year we had been waiting for.

Swimming had become so popular that it was used as a marketing tool in Mission Viejo to promote the city. I think that's how they got President Ford to come to Mission Viejo to speak on the city's tenth anniversary in May of 1976. As two of the leading stars in the swimming program, Brian Goodell and I were invited to meet the president. I dug out the camera I'd gotten at the 1972 Olympics four years earlier and headed to Mission Viejo High School, which was where President Ford would be speaking. One of the Secret Service men stopped me at the door and made me take a picture with my camera, to see if the flashcube had an explosive device in it.

"Being a swimmer myself," President Ford said in his speech, "I'm impressed by the number of championship swimmers that Mission Viejo produces. And I'm gambling that you will prove it again in the Olympic Trials this summer."

The fact that the Olympics were taking place in the year of the United States Bicentennial seemed to make them even more significant. The Bicentennial celebration was everywhere. It had started the year before, in 1975, when the American Freedom Train was launched in Wilmington, Delaware, beginning a tour of all forty-eight contiguous states. Celebrations were happening everywhere in anticipation of the nation's twentieth birthday. Red, white, and blue seemed to cover everything. The fact that we would be swimming in Montreal just a few weeks after the July 4 celebrations was not lost on us. If there were ever a year to step up and deliver for our country, this was it.

"Back in '72, I was just an excited kid in Munich," I said to Mark one day at practice. "I didn't really get what it meant to be representing your country. But I get it now. I want to go out there and not just win a gold medal, but also hear our national anthem playing. I want to represent my country with pride and dignity."

Mark understood. "I know you do, Shirley," he said. "I get it. You know what makes the Olympics different from other competitions."

I truly did. At the time, I was swimming so many meets that many of them remain a blur. Of course, the big ones will usually stand out in your memory, but many of them are connected as one seamless and endless series of races. I'll read articles today about certain competitions, or even breaking records, and have no memory of them whatsoever. There were just too many. But the Olympics were different, and the 1976 Games were going to be something special.

One day, after practice in Mission Viejo, a bunch of us were hanging around in Mark's office, as we would sometimes do. As usual, I was sitting in his chair behind his desk, spinning it around while we all made small talk and waited for Mark. One of the guys, a swimmer from Puerto Rico named Jesse Vassallo, said to no one in particular, "Wouldn't it be cool if there were a pill we could all take so we wouldn't have to practice?"

The rest of us looked at him, surprised.

"Yeah," he continued. "It would make you so strong that you would never have to practice, you'd just go out there and swim your races."

"But that would defeat the purpose of working for something," I said to him.

He shrugged and laughed. "Yeah, I guess so," he said. "I was just thinking. We practice so hard every day that it would be kind of cool if there were something that did that for us."

For the next few minutes, we debated what it would be like if we could cheat by taking a pill that would make us stronger. And one by one, we all agreed that it would be a bad idea, that we were out there swimming for a reason, and that we actually cared about practicing, as hard as it sometimes was, because it was the right way to do things.

I knew Jesse didn't really mean anything by it. He was a few years younger than me and was just thinking out loud. He went on to become an amazing swimmer, competing at the 1984 Olympic Games and then going on to become the first Puerto Rican to be inducted into the International Swimming Hall of Fame.

That spring, I started getting tired of being asked, wherever I went, how it felt to be going up against the East Germans. I would tell all the writers, "We have a very strong team. It's not just about me." But the media was looking for drama and continued to pit me against the country of East Germany. There's already enough pressure when you go to the Olympics; you're competing against many different countries. But when the media makes it about you and one other country, that's something completely different. It made me very uncomfortable. I remember one headline that said I was "virtually a one-girl U.S. team holding back the East German flood." Another article in the *Sports Illustrated* Olympic preview issue read: "She bears on her tanned shoulders the full burden of the U.S.'s proud tradition in women's swimming." The pressure was on.

One day, about a month before the Olympic Trials in Long Beach, it all came to a head. I sort of snapped. For the first time in four years, I skipped practice.

I decided to quit swimming.

I didn't sit there giving it a ton of thought. It just got to a point where, in an emotional moment, I thought, I don't want to do this anymore. Everything just caught up with me. Swimming twenty miles a day, every day, was so much work. I wasn't working toward beating the East Germans; I was working to represent my country in the best way I could. But everybody was so busy shaping and molding the narrative around me that, as a brash nineteen-year-old, I just decided that was it. I was done.

I then did what plenty of other teenage girls would have done on a beautiful, early summer day. I went to the beach. All by myself, with just a towel, I rode my bicycle down to Huntington Beach and spent a lazy day swimming and lying in the sun. It was heavenly. I had forgotten what it was like to just zone out and not think about anything. This is how normal people live, I thought to myself. How nice to have this kind of freedom, with no pressure.

As I looked out over the waves by the pier, I thought back to a few years earlier, when I swam in contests to see who could circle the pier fastest. I always won. In fact, I'd get so far out in front of everyone that I'd be by myself out in the ocean, beyond the pier.

But today, I wasn't racing. I didn't have to worry about anything. There was no pressure. I thought about Shane Gould, and how she had retired at seventeen. I hadn't really understood her decision back in 1973, but now I could relate—the press played a huge part in it. I envied the peace and solitude Shane must have had, now that she was retired.

After a couple of hours, I walked over to Dwight's, the oldest beach concession stand in Huntington Beach, and ordered myself a big plate of "strips and cheese," a locally invented surfer snack consisting of tortilla chips, shredded cheddar cheese, and salsa. I was in heaven. I ate my snack back on my towel, swam, tanned a little more, and then called it a day.

I rode my bike back home as the sun went down and was shocked to see Mark's blue Porsche parked outside our home when I got there. Uh-oh, I thought. When I walked into the living room and saw him sitting there on our couch with my mom, I didn't know what to say. Mark asked me where I'd been.

"I can't take it anymore," I told him. "I think I'm just going to quit. There's too much pressure and I'm tired of it. I need a break from all of this."

Mark got up off the couch and asked me to go outside with him. He told my mom that we would be back in a little while. We got into his Porsche and he just drove around the neighborhood, talking to me calmly and reassuringly.

"Shirley," he said, " I understand what it's like to feel the weight of the world on your shoulders. I don't think it's fair that the media has put you in this position. But I also know that I don't want you to be known as the girl who gave up. Because you're not a quitter. You're a champion. You have an incredible opportunity in front of you, and I want you to get a fair shot at it."

Mark told me that he was going to keep everyone away from me and create a protected environment for me leading into the Olympic Trials. He just wanted me to focus on swimming, without any distractions or added pressure.

"You've worked so hard these last few years," he said. "You know how hard you've worked. That's all you should be thinking about. Not the East Germans or the press. You just focus on your swimming, okay?"

"That's what I've wanted to do all along," I said. "I don't like all the attention. I just want to swim."

"I'll protect you," Mark said. "You focus on the upcoming Trials. Then you focus on the Olympics. As long as you're with me, they will not be able to get to you. Okay?"

Who could argue with that? Mark was an amazing coach. I was just being emotional, but he took what I was doing very seriously. We drove back to my house, and I gathered up my gear and headed to practice with Mark. When I got in the pool, some of the other kids looked at me like they wanted to ask where I had been, but nobody said anything.

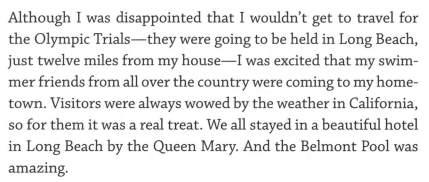

Although I was disappointed that I wouldn't get to travel for the Olympic Trials—they were going to be held in Long Beach, just twelve miles from my house—I was excited that my swimmer friends from all over the country were coming to my hometown. Visitors were always wowed by the weather in California, so for them it was a real treat. We all stayed in a beautiful hotel in Long Beach by the Queen Mary. And the Belmont Pool was amazing.

For me, the differences between the '72 and '76 Trials were very noticeable. I was only fifteen years old at the '72 Trials, so I hadn't really known what I was getting into or how important the meet was. Four years later, at age nineteen, I knew exactly what was going on. It was still fun and exciting, but I now knew who was behind the curtain: the Iron Curtain. Just a few weeks earlier at their Trials, the East German women's team had shattered a slew of world records, which raised new suspicions in my mind. What was going on over there?

Back in 1973, the East Germans' record-breaking times had been really strange. But now, it was just what they did. There was nothing shocking about it anymore. In a way, seeing the times that they were swimming made me more aggressive; it pushed me. To me, the East German women's times were just like the times of those guys I swam against in college. That's what I was swimming against. Guys.

The first event I swam in at the Trials was my favorite—the 200 freestyle. It wasn't too long or too short. Jill Sterkel, Kim Peyton, and my friend Kathy were my closest competition. My goal was to break the two-minute mark, but it didn't happen. Still, I swam my fastest time of 2:00.69 and set a new American record.

The next event was the 400 individual medley, two lengths each of the butterfly, backstroke, breaststroke, and freestyle. Although I swam mostly freestyle, I liked the individual medley because each stroke was a different story. Someone could be way ahead at the end of the butterfly and totally inept at the breaststroke. Being average at the majority of the strokes but strong at freestyle gave me another win.

Next was the 400 freestyle, another favorite of mine. I went out extremely slow for the first 200 meters. At the 200-foot turn, there was one girl in front of me, and the crowd was going crazy. I turned up the speed and the crowd got quiet as I qualified first. I was in perfect condition at the perfect time.

In the finals that night, three good things happened. I made my best time and set another American record, and my good friend Kathy made the Olympic team.

The following day was the 100-meter freestyle, which was not my favorite race because it was over in less than a minute. It required no strategy or pacing, just an all-out sprint. I did my best time and set another American record. The freestyle relay was now set for the Olympics, with the top four finishers in place. Jill was second, Kim third, and Wendy Boglioli fourth. We talked on the deck for a few minutes about how cool it was that we would be swimming together as a team. But really, we had no idea that in Montreal, we would become part of something so special that our names would live together forever. Kim said to me, "I think we'll make a good team. I have a good feeling about this relay team."

The last event was the 800-meter free. I was pretty confident that I was going to win. I didn't pay much attention to who was challenging me. All I had to do was pace myself and win my own race.

Not long before it was time to swim the 800, I got really hungry. I knew there was a Jack in the Box across the street from the pool, so I snuck out without telling anybody and walked over there by myself. I got myself a Jumbo Jack, fries, and a Coke, brought it all back to the pool, and wolfed it all down. Someone walking by looked at me and said, "Wow, that's what you eat?" Did they think I was on a diet or something? Back then, I could eat pretty much whatever I wanted. When you're swimming twenty miles a day, it doesn't really matter what you eat, because you are burning so many calories. You might as well enjoy whatever you want.

After I touched the wall at the end of the 800, I knew I had won. The cheering was so loud. I jumped out of the water, and Mark was right there to shake my hand. I was extremely happy that the East Germans would know I had beat them.

This wound up being my greatest performance to date. Winning every freestyle event and the 400-meter individual medley was all the evidence I needed that Mark's training was continuing to pay off. At the Trials, I set three U.S. records in the heats and three more in the finals, and then broke the world record in the 800-meter freestyle. On my way off the pool deck that day, I overheard a writer say to somebody, "That was one of the greatest swimming performances in history." I was feeling good, and I'd sent a message back to East Germany.

No matter what they were doing to their bodies, I was ready to take them on. I was ready to fight.

I read the *Long Beach Press-Telegram* the next day, and the report was very positive:

> *Shirley Babashoff had a tremendous overall performance at the United States Olympic Swimming Trials Monday night by smashing both the existing world record and the pending mark in the women's 800-meter freestyle with a time of 8:39.63 seconds. The nineteen-year-old swimming queen from Fountain Valley, California, bettered the pending mark of 8:40.68 set by East Germany's Petra Thümer in the communist nation's trials at East Berlin on June 4. "They opened the door and we can do better," Ms. Babashoff said of the record time set by the East German woman. . . . Shirley Babashoff showed nearly unprecedented versatility. At the trials she won the 100, 200, 400, and 800-meter freestyles as well as the 400 IM. The only event where she was remotely challenged was the 100 free, where eventual American record holder Jill Sterkel would finish second by .29. Each of her freestyle swims were American records, with the 800 also a world record. Babashoff left the Trials with a buzz surrounding the possibility of a female "Spitz" who could win a possible 7 golds at the Games.*

Reporters had asked me the day before if I had any objection to being referred to as a female Mark Spitz. I told them, "Nobody is as good as Mark Spitz." And I meant that.

Just before I left for training camp, I read this in the *Mission Viejo Reporter*:

> *Between winning races and breaking records at the Olympics Swim Trial held two weeks ago in Long Beach, Mission Viejo Nadadore Shirley Babashoff made it clear that she*

cares as much about defeating the East German distaffers at the Montreal Olympics as she does about winning medals.

"I guess you could say that the East Germans have kind of helped me along," said Babashoff, referring to the Germans' recent world record-smashing performance at their Olympics Trials. "They've set some goals for me to work for."

Babashoff, who is undeniably the cream of America's mermaids, will get plenty of chances to combat the East Germans in Montreal. She is entered in five individual and two relay events at the Games, more than any other American athlete, and in each one she will face stiff challenges from the East German girls.

CHAPTER ELEVEN

Training for '76

Our training camp was at West Point Military Academy, up in the pretty country north of New York City. The choice of venue for the woman's swim team seemed rather idiotic. All those cute guys and a bunch of teenaged girls? We were to be there for three weeks. My brother, Jack, would be swimming in these Olympics, too, but the men's team was training elsewhere.

Once again, the coach who had gotten me there, Mark, wasn't allowed to be there for the most important races of my life. Today, the rules are different and your coach can accompany you, in large part thanks to later efforts by Mark.

I flew to New York City, and our team bus took us up along the pretty Hudson River into the beautiful country where the famed academy was located. The day I arrived, I opened the *Los Angeles Times* in the cafeteria and saw this headline above an article:

CADETS FALL IN LOVE WITH QUEEN SHIRLEY

It was kind of funny how the writer, well-known columnist Skip Bayless, captured what I was going through at the time. Training at West Point was something I'll never forget. Dealing with the media at the academy was absolute insanity. Without

Mark there, my first line of protection was gone. Bayless's article began:

> *The call has gone through a harried hotel operator, the assistant coach, the coach, and a recording machine. When final high security clearances are given, Queen Shirley's line is busy. Click. Automatic transfer back to Jack Nelson, coach of the women's Olympic swimming team training at West Point.*

After my performance at the Olympic Trials in Long Beach, it seemed as if the entire world was waiting for nothing else but me versus the East Germans. It was all of the pressure that had forced me to quit a few months earlier, times 1,000. But by now, I was ready to deal with it. In fact, I was even enjoying it a little bit because I felt so good about my performance as a swimmer. I also felt that I had much to prove against the East Germans who, in my opinion, were clearly doing something suspicious.

Some of these things came through in Bayless's article. But mostly, it was just another chance for a writer to start analyzing my behavior, even when I was just being my blunt and honest self. When Bayless finally got me on the telephone line, I explained that I had just been out in the hallway, playing around.

"You guys won't let me be a normal nineteen-year-old girl," I added. "It's like it's going to be Shirley versus the world in Montreal, and you put so much pressure on me that sometimes I feel like screaming."

Bayless also wrote:

> *Since the '72 Olympics, some writers have found shy little Shirley to be big surly Shirley. As records fell in her wake, she seemed more and more aloof. Her smile, always Mona Lisa crooked, appeared to be a scowl. Her laugh, before quick and warm, seemed rusty. Her obsession for supremacy had*

curtailed her bike riding, softball and volleyball playing, and body surfing. All work and no play made Shirley a very cranky girl.

"Surly Shirley." That's what I got for being so dedicated to my sport. Something tells me that if Mr. Bayless had been writing about a male athlete, it may have been presented a little bit differently. I would not have been "surly," but probably "steadfast." My laugh may not have been "rusty," but rather "rugged."

From competing against boys during practice for all those years and essentially only swimming with boys, my attitude had become more serious and gruff. That was my discipline. There was no way around it. But rather than looking at the complexity of my swimming practices and how they may have affected my life and attitude, many writers decided to take the lazy route and write me off as cranky.

Well, they weren't going to get me down in Montreal. I was too fired up and ready to win. By that point, I had globe-trotted through dozens of countries, swam in dozens of competitions, and become a more dedicated swimmer. I had grown a lot from the fresh-faced kid I'd been at the '72 Games. But the media was not allowing me to grow up. They had created a false mold for me to fit into, based on every other Olympian who had come before me.

At training camp, I really didn't like the head coach, Jack Nelson. He struck me as less of a coach and more of a grandstanding PR guy. He was always bolstering his own image and taking credit for things that he had little to do with. I had never even met him before training at West Point, yet all of the sudden he was speaking for me and taking credit for my achievements. He was blustery and seemed very full of himself. Not my style, but there was nothing I could do about it.

The practices were terrible, too. Hardly any thought at all

was given to them. We were told, "Just swim ten 400s." That was it. I was not allowed to swim one stroke of the butterfly, breaststroke, or backstroke either. Also, our relay team never even swam any practice runs together. At Knoxville in '72, our relay team swam world record times at practice so we knew how we would do at the Olympics. At West Point, no such rehearsal ever took place. If Mark knew about this, I thought to myself, he'd go nuts. Given how pointless most of the actual "training" was, I kept to myself as much as I could.

I had qualified to swim in the individual medley, but I was never allowed to swim anything but freestyle at camp. At one practice, Nelson came onto the pool deck and said, "Today we're going to swim eight 1,500s. Shirley, you go first and everyone else follow."

I got about 400 meters in and then got out of the pool. Those practices were not going to help anyone, so I just said I felt sick and left the pool. I didn't want to waste my time.

One of the other coaches, Frank Elm, was also my friend Kathy's coach back home. "Is he always like this?" I asked her. She shook her head and said that, back home, he ran regular practices. She didn't know why our training was so bad—why there just wasn't any strategy to it.

I did enjoy our last night at West Point, though. Crandal Pool, where we were training, was opened up to the public and we all put on a show for the locals. It was a really fun exhibition. We swam practice relays and entertained the crowd of about 1,500 fans who had turned up to watch us swim and wish us well as we got ready to head north for the Games.

When it was time to break camp, our plan was to pack everything up and head north to the State University of New York at

Plattsburgh, where we would meet up with the other athletes and get our Olympic warm-up suits and other official clothing. We would then caravan across the Canadian border into Montreal.

There was a ton of excitement once we reached Plattsburgh. I saw my brother, Jack, along with some other friends including Brian Goodell and John Naber. We got our warm-ups along with all of the other goodies: cameras, goggles, swimsuits, duffle bags, pens, and, of course, the much-sought-after Olympic trading pins that both athletes and fans liked to swap.

On my first day there, a U.S. Olympic official asked me if I would like to pose for the cover of *Sports Illustrated*. I was stunned. Of course I would—who wouldn't? Apparently, as he explained, a lot of people.

"Look," he said, "it might sound crazy, but a lot of athletes talk about the 'curse' of appearing on the cover of *Sports Illustrated* before the Games. I guess a lot of people have underperformed after being on the cover."

I'm not superstitious, so that sounded crazy to me. I was thrilled and honored to be asked. It's true that I was getting tired of the media hounding me, but the cover of *Sports Illustrated* was different. So, later that day, I was led out to the bleachers at the school's football stadium and met basketball player Scott May and Frank Shorter, the legendary long-distance runner who had won a gold in 1972. They were both awesome guys, really friendly, and we had a great time posing for the photographer in our brand-new, red Team USA jackets.

What really struck me about those two guys was just how much they loved their respective sports. That's all they talked about during the photo shoot. You have to remember, there was no money back then. You didn't do any of this to get rich. You did it because you simply loved and respected your sport and the idea of competition. So most people were usually happy to do things like pose for magazine covers. It was just a really nice perk in the midst of all the hard work.

Another treat they had scheduled for us was a visit from the president of the United States, Gerald Ford. Plattsburgh hadn't had a presidential visit since Franklin D. Roosevelt visited in 1939. But given that the small city was the staging area for us before we headed to the Games, it made sense for him to visit us there and wish us well.

He arrived on July 10 at the Plattsburgh Air Force Base, where more than 10,000 people waited to watch Air Force One land. We had noticed Secret Service agents around our dorms in Plattsburgh a day or two before the president arrived. When his official presidential limousine pulled up, all of the athletes joined him onstage in front of the Plattsburgh Field House to hear his speech along with thousands gathered out front. A huge banner hung over the stage: Plattsburgh Salutes 1976 Olympic Team.

This was part of the speech President Ford gave on that warm and humid afternoon:

*I have always had a great interest in athletics. It goes back a good many years. I was looking at a book on the way up here—a friend of mine gave it to me—*The History of the Olympics. *And I was thumbing through the various Olympics that were held for a good many years, and the ones that I remember go back to, well, about 1924, 1928. I always had a great ambition that was never fulfilled because I was not good enough.*

I remember the names of Eddie Tolan, Jesse Owens, and a good many of the others who set great records in those days. But the competition gets tougher every four years, which is the way the world is. And all of you have great opportunities to do better than those who have come before you, and I know you will because you have the right desire and you worked hard. Let me say you have the 100 percent support of the American people. . . .

That is a great way for us to enter our third century. That is a century all of you are really going to live in and work in and help to make a better America. And the job that you are going to do up there in Montreal, where you are going to run faster, jump higher, shoot better, swim better, do all the things that you have been training for a long time— you will have the full and wholehearted support of 215 million Americans, including your president, who will be darn proud of you. The very best to you.

Listening to President Ford's words reminded me of just how proud I was to be representing my country. That's the thing about the Olympics. Wherever you went and whatever you did, you never forgot that you were there on behalf of the United States. It was almost like being an ambassador. I took it very seriously; it meant a lot to me to be representing my country. I always felt that Americans would appreciate someone who was honest and didn't hold back. That I would be accepted just as I was.

After the president finished his speech, he made his way through the crowd of athletes during a special reception. Everybody crushed in, trying to get close to him. Since I had already met him in California a couple of months earlier, I was happy to let others get closer and have their moment. It was exciting to watch the leader of the free world interact with these young and excited athletes from so many different countries.

Suddenly, I heard President Ford call out, "Where is Shirley Babashoff? Does anybody know where Shirley Babashoff is?"

Was I really hearing him right? It was surreal to hear the president of the United States saying my name and wondering where I was.

The crowd around me pushed me toward him, and a couple of athletes around me said, "Mr. President, she's right here! She's right over here!" With that, President Ford turned around and approached me with a warm smile.

"Shirley," he said kindly. "It's so good to see you again."

I had no clue what to say except, "You too, Mr. President."

He looked me directly in the eye and wished me luck. Then he asked me how many events I would be swimming in up in Montreal. I told him I'd be participating in seven.

"Ah," he grinned. "Just like that guy Jack Spitz."

I nodded. "Yes, just like Jack Spitz." Hey, this was the president of the United States, and I was not about to correct him. I was still amazed that he even remembered me.

Just a couple of hours after the reception, buses and vans began filling up with athletes for the caravan to Montreal. As my teammates and I headed toward one of the tour buses, an Olympic official tapped my shoulder and said, "No, Shirley, you're not riding on the bus. You're riding in the number-one van."

Evidently, they were transporting a few of the more high-profile athletes separately from the rest of the teams. I was taken to a van with one other athlete sitting in it—track and field star Bruce Jenner. It seemed that he and I would be riding in the van alone, along with a pair of Olympic officials.

"Hey," I said to him as I got into the seat across the aisle from him. He barely acknowledged me. I had never met Bruce before, but I knew at that moment that for the duration of the sixty-mile journey, there wasn't going to be much conversation. He pretty much acted as if I were invisible.

Looking out the window along the journey, I noticed how it almost felt like a presidential motorcade was heading up Interstate 87 toward the border. Thruway on-ramps were closed as our caravan roared past, and hundreds of people along the overpasses were waving flags and banners, wishing us the best of luck. It was fun to wave to all the people who were lining the roadways to wish us well.

"Isn't this great?" I asked Bruce.

No reaction.

"Should be pretty exciting, huh?"

Silence.

"Feeling good about the decathlon?"

Nothing. Oh well.

I really appreciated that those people had come out to support us. It was a beautiful show of spirit that I thought would give everyone an extra boost of confidence. It reminded me once more just how much the Olympics meant to people and why it was so important to do our best at the Games. It was just so different than any other competition. There was so much at stake.

CHAPTER TWELVE

The Montreal Games

When we arrived in Montreal, the first thing I noticed was how much tighter the security was than it had been four years earlier in Munich. After the catastrophic Munich massacre at last year's Games, it was now impossible for the public to come anywhere near the Olympic dorms. Security fences surrounded everything. All of the fans who were hoping to trade Olympic pins or get autographs were now kept outside the gates, which made it safer for us, but more of a challenge for them. Even the buses we rode had armed guards on them.

I also noticed how unfinished a lot of the facilities looked. There were no window coverings on many of the apartments where the athletes would be staying. There was a lot of un-painted concrete, and there were cranes looming near some of the venues. It was a stark contrast to how buttoned-up Munich had been. It seemed as if they needed a few more months to finish everything up.

Once we had entered the Village and dragged our suitcases up to our rooms, the attitude seemed to change among us athletes. I overheard a couple of the girls talking and wasn't surprised to hear that they were already worrying about the East German swimmers. That scared me. I knew very well that you couldn't let your opponents get to your head. If anything, you wanted to get into *their* head. I had become pretty good at that. So while I could sympathize a bit with their fears about the East German team, I didn't really have any patience for it.

I told the girls to stop worrying about the East Germans. We had a great team, and we needed to act like it. "We may not know exactly what they are doing, but we can't let them intimidate us," I said. No matter what I said, though, I could tell it was still eating away at them.

I was the only person on our team to get her own room. Between this and riding in the private van up from Plattsburgh, I felt a little spoiled. I think the U.S. Olympic officials were doing what they could to coddle who they thought were their most promising or even star athletes. It didn't really matter to me, though. We all hung out together and treated each other as equals. Nobody was better than anybody else, and more often than not, a lot of the girls hung out in my room anyway.

The day we arrived, we had to take a sex test to prove that we were actually women. Instead of yanking out a piece of my hair like they had done in Munich, the nurses swabbed the inside of my cheek. Much less painful. They actually gave us each a little card to make it official. I wondered how the East Germans had passed the test, but then I figured that whatever they were doing was probably so advanced, it could outsmart any testing.

My teammates and I were excited to see the pool. We knew it was going to be something special. We hopped on the bus, which took us through a special underground tunnel and dropped us off at an athletes-only entrance. That was unique. At our meets, we usually just got off the bus at the public entrance and went through the front doors like everybody else. But in Montreal—maybe as a result of what had happened to the Israeli athletes four years earlier—it seemed like the security was going to be much more intense. That said, there was still a gaggle of reporters and photographers waiting for us when we got off the bus.

We entered the venue in awe. The building was incredible. It was designed by French architect Roger Taillibert, who had also designed the Olympic Stadium and Village. It held more than 10,000 people and looked beautiful and futuristic, similar to the Olympic Stadium we had just passed on the bus and the Velodrome, where the cycling competitions would be held. As we wandered through the beautiful structure, I know everyone was imagining what it would be like to swim there when the place was packed with screaming fans.

We were eager to change into our swimsuits so we could get into the water and check things out. From what I could tell up on the deck, the Montreal pool was perfectly designed. But there are many factors to take into consideration when you're swimming in a pool you've never been in before. What's the water like? Is it cold or warm? Is it "crispy"? Is it "creamy"? Those terms might sound odd, but serious swimmers can sense these things; every swimmer feels the water differently. How is the pool actually designed? Will the water be choppy? Will there be waves? Will there be a sharp smell of chlorine?

Me and my two friends and teammates, Kathy and Camille, went into the locker room to change into our swimsuits. Just like everything else, the locker room was really nice and had these tall lockers that prevented you from seeing anybody beyond your own row.

As we were getting changed, we suddenly heard deep voices fill the room. There were men talking in another language just on the other side of our lockers! The three of us were completely naked, so we freaked out and started screaming. We threw our clothes back on, gathered up our gear, and ran out of the locker room as fast as we could.

When we got back out on the deck, we bumped into a few

swimmers from the American men's team and we told them
what had happened.

"Are these unisex locker rooms?" I asked one of them. Some
international meets actually have those, so it wasn't out of the
question.

"No," he told me. "That was the ladies locker room you were
just in."

That's when we saw them come out. One by one, the girls
from the East German team filed out of the locker room. We
stared at them in amazement. They looked very different from
the last time I had seen them, in Colombia the year before.
Their muscles were huge, even bigger than they had been before. They walked funny. A couple of them even seemed to have
the beginnings of mustaches. It was bizarre.

As they walked past us, we could hear them talking. The
voices sounded unmistakably male. They had been the ones
with the deep voices in the locker room.

They lumbered past us without even acknowledging anyone. My teammates and I looked at each other in disbelief. This
was beyond creepy. From Belgrade to Concord to Cali and finally to Montreal, they had progressively become more and more
like men.

We went back into the locker room to change and then did a
couple of laps to get a sense of the water. The pool was amazing.
It was perfect. But I couldn't get those "girls" out of my mind.
What the hell had happened to Kornelia Ender? Looking at her
across the pool, I couldn't even believe it was her. Weightlifting
was one thing, but there was nothing I knew of that could have
given her those broad shoulders and thunder thighs.

After swimming for a while, we dried off, put on our sweats,
and headed toward the bus. By this time, even more reporters
were loitering at the door, waiting to fire off questions at us as
we left. As I made my way to the bus, I was faced with a flurry

of flashbulbs, microphones, and questions.

"Shirley, Shirley! What do you think of the East German team?"

"What's your opinion of the East German team?"

"What can you tell us about the East German team?"

The questions were all redundant and overlapping. But I stopped for a moment and said into one of the reporters' microphones, "Well, except for their deep voices and mustaches, I think they'll probably do fine."

I saw some eyes widen and a couple of jaws drop. The reporters then fired off a couple of follow-up questions, which I answered basically the same way. Then I got on the bus and went back to the Village to have dinner with my teammates.

Honestly, I had no idea that all hell would break loose after I made those comments about the East Germans. The reporters ran to file their stories and before I had even swum in a race, there was talk about how "Surly Shirley" was being a poor sport. According to the press, I was bad-mouthing the poor German girls who, as everyone knew, had become extra strong from their high-altitude training and extra fast due to their specially designed swimsuits. Yeah. Right.

As an Olympic athlete, I did have the advantage of being protected inside the bubble of the Village. It wasn't like I was watching the news every night or reading the papers. I didn't care about any of that stuff. All I cared about was focusing on the races that were coming up in a few days. I was unaware of the firestorm my comments had created—for now, anyway.

The day after we arrived, I was thrilled to see my coach, Mark, who was there working as a coach for the Uruguay team, but it was really just a way for him to be there for me. I told him about the terrible training sessions at West Point, and how I wasn't allowed to swim the breaststroke or butterfly or backstroke. He was furious.

"I told those coaches what they had to do with you," he said. "I wrote out exactly what you need to do in preparation for everything. How can they expect you to swim the 400 individual medley without having practiced any of those strokes for the last several weeks?"

I couldn't have agreed with him more. I'd been concerned about it for weeks. I knew I wasn't ready to swim in the 400, so I asked Mark to pull me out. Although it created a lot of controversy, I felt that it was the right decision. "Why did you wait so long?" people asked me. But once I explained the situation, they understood. Now I would be swimming in six races instead of seven.

Meanwhile, word had continued to spread about my comments regarding the East Germans. It got so bad that the American Olympic officials sent flowers to the East German team, to apologize for my words. Had I known they were going to do this, I wouldn't have said anything at all. All of the sudden, people started to keep their distance from me, as if I'd become toxic or radioactive. All I had done was state an observation. I knew that everybody was aware of what I was talking about and, for the most part, agreed that something really strange was going on. But nobody else said anything. This was the Olympics, and you didn't do things like that. You didn't speak your mind. You followed protocol, and that was it.

The media didn't investigate my comments about the East German team; in fact, the reporters couldn't even find them. That's because the team wasn't even staying at the Olympic Village. Instead, they were reportedly tucked away on a boat, out of reach and out of sight.

Thankfully, not all of the media was broadcasting bad

things about me. ABC Sports had already prepared a long feature about me, which they had shot back home in Huntington Beach. They had filmed me riding my bike along the ocean and documented various aspects of my life. They had done the same thing with Kornelia Ender, creating two mini-documentaries that pitted us against each other by juxtaposing just how different our worlds were. The great swimmer Donna de Varona was also working as a sportscaster at the Olympics, and she conducted several positive and fair interviews with me throughout the course of the Games.

It was the international writers who seemed to have it in for me, after I made those comments about the East Germans. They never wasted an opportunity to criticize me, mock me, or speculate that my anger was based on nothing more than my own insecurity and lack of confidence. That could not have been further from the truth. I may have had teammates who were intimidated by the East Germans, but I was more than ready to do battle.

Behind the scenes, my teammates fully supported me being outspoken about the East German team. In fact, they loved it.

"Go get 'em, Shirley," one of them whispered.

"I wish I had your guts," said another.

I tried to stay occupied during my downtime. Despite what was going on in the press, life within the Village was fun. Just like in 1972, there were many different ways for us to entertain ourselves—everything from listening rooms with all the latest albums and a great stereo to a miniature golf course.

Because of the notoriety I had achieved at that point, it was hard for me to walk around outside the Village without getting mobbed for autographs, especially if I wore my USA sweatsuit.

Eventually, it just became impossible to go anywhere in public. But still, there were some nights that we were able to sneak out and explore Montreal under the radar, which was really nice.

A day or so before the Games actually started, the Canadian singer Gordon Lightfoot gave a special private concert for the athletes in the Olympic Village. The performance was held in a little courtyard. I decided to go by myself to hear him sing. I enjoyed his music and thought it might be a nice way to clear my head before all the competitions started.

It was a nice little perk for us athletes to have someone of his stature give us our own show, and I was surprised that hardly anybody was there to hear him sing. A small stage was set up, probably not even more than a foot high, and I was sitting literally right next to him as he performed. The songs were beautiful, and they filled the cool night air with warmth. At one point, he remarked that he was a bit chilly. Since I was so close to him, I asked him if he'd like to wear my warm-up jacket. He smiled at me and said, "That's okay, love. I'll be okay, but thank you." He seemed very charming and for the few of us who showed up to hear him play, it certainly made for a special night.

My parents were also able to come to Montreal for the Games (my dad was on work release). Athletes were entitled to some complimentary tickets, and I had given my parents some of them. Rather than actually using all of the tickets, my parents scalped the extras before I even swam a race. It's no secret that plenty of other people were doing this; I'd seen the same thing happen in Munich back in 1972.

Two days before the start of the Games, I met my parents outside the Village. They were breathless and excited.

"Shirley, you'll never believe this," they said. "You'll never believe who wants to talk to you."

"Who?" I asked.

"O. J.!" my father gushed.

I had no idea who that was. I didn't pay attention to any other sports besides swimming. I was sort of cut off from most of the world, given my practice schedule. The name was a bit familiar, but I couldn't have told you anything about O. J. Simpson.

"He's the most famous football player on earth," my father told me impatiently. "He's a sportscaster now, and he really wants to talk to you about the Olympics. We spoke to him and he is very excited at the opportunity to meet you."

It was obvious that my father was just excited about the opportunity to meet one of his favorite football players. It didn't seem like that big of a deal to me.

My father explained that O. J. wanted to meet me at the swimming arena. So, later that day, I wandered over to the arena at the appointed time, expecting to find O. J. and a camera crew from ABC Sports.

But I was in for a surprise. When I arrived, the venue was all but empty and there, lingering by himself in one of the seats about halfway up the grandstand, sat a good-looking guy. He waved me up and introduced himself as O. J. Simpson.

It was kind of an odd scene. I said hello and was expecting to hear that he was there to interview me about the upcoming races. But instead, O. J. just made small talk and even seemed to be flirting a little bit. Finally, he seemed to get a bit frustrated, as I wasn't picking up on much of what he was saying.

"Do you even know who I am?" he asked me. "Do you know who O. J. Simpson is?"

"Sorry," I said. "I know my dad's a big fan, but I've never really heard of you. But did you want to do an interview with me?"

With that, he got up and walked down the stairs and out of the arena. I guess he was expecting something a little different from what he got.

The opening ceremonies for the Games were on July 17, and I watched them in my apartment on closed-circuit television. I had been advised to pass on the ceremonies, since it was the day before my first race. I hated to miss them, but I had seen them in Munich and understood what they were all about. Tonight, I needed my sleep. My schedule was going to be tight, with my first race on July 18, the next on July 19, another on July 20, one on July 22, and two on July 25.

As soon as the opening ceremonies ended, I killed the lights and went to sleep. I had a big week ahead.

CHAPTER THIRTEEN

Forming a Strategy

The next day, I competed in the 4x100 medley relay with my teammates Linda Jezek, Lauri Siering, and Camille Wright. We were anxious and excited, but we felt ready.

We got crushed. The East Germans recorded a time of 4:07.95, a full 5.5 seconds better than the listed world record, and 6.6 seconds ahead of us. We won the silver, and Canada won the bronze.

This first race was an eye opener. The East Germans were swimming ridiculous times, and they didn't even seem winded at the end of the race. It was so obvious that something was going on. I couldn't even look the team in the eye when we received our medals moments later.

The media was beside itself about the performance. Were they blind? The East Germans' muscle structure was ridiculous. Of course, the press wrote about how annoyed I looked while receiving my silver medal.

I saw Mark after the race and expressed my frustration to him. He agreed but told me that right now, there was nothing that could be done. I had to go out there and keep swimming my best. I knew he was right, but it all seemed so wrong.

"You all swam great times," he said. "Just swim your hardest."

The next event was the 100 freestyle. Kornelia Ender had won this race at the 1973 and 1975 World Championships, and had set nine world records in the 100 frees since the Munich Olympics. Because of this, she came into Montreal as the favorite.

Sure enough, Ender won the race. Her winning time was her tenth consecutive world record in the 100 free, finishing in 55.65. It was the fifth time she had bettered 56 seconds, and she was the only woman to do so at the time. Behind her for the silver was her teammate Petra Priemer, followed by the Netherlands' Enith Brigitha (a win that made Brigitha the first black swimmer to win an Olympic medal). I came in fifth.

After a couple of the races, I refused to shake the East Germans' hands. Of course, this made for some splashy headlines. "How could Shirley Babashoff treat the East German athletes like this?" some writers wondered in their articles. My question was, how could the East Germans treat the rest of the world like this? I was swimming some of the best times in my life, times that I had worked hard to achieve. But to no avail. It was frustrating, to say the least.

Some people might say, look, this is the Olympics and you've got to uphold the spirit of sportsmanship, especially when you don't have any specific scientific evidence to expose the East Germans. I understand that argument. But you have to understand what it's like to be a trained athlete. There are certain things that are physically impossible, and that's what I was witnessing; that's what everyone was witnessing. There was no way the East Germans could have improved as much as they had without some sort of help. It went way beyond high-altitude training, special swimsuits, and testing blood.

Imagine that you're at your job, and somebody comes in with no experience and cheats you out of what you have worked so hard for. Would you shake their hand and say to them, "Hey,

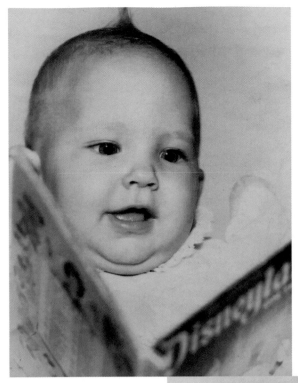

As a baby in 1957.

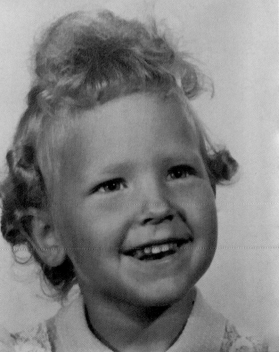

At three years old, long
before I ever set foot in a
swimming pool, circa 1960.

i

Christmas, circa 1962, with my father, Jack, my brothers, Bill and Jack Jr.,
and my mother, Vera.

Our tradition of splashing our coach, Don Lamont, in the pool after a meet, circa 1966.

Playing with a gyroscope toy—one of the ways I'd kill time between races—circa 1967.

Waiting for the starting gun at age ten (*second from right*), circa 1967.

With a first-place trophy for the backstroke in 1967.

With my teammates—including Sandy Neilson (*middle right*) and Cozette Wheeler (*far right*)—at the Belmont Plaza pool in Long Beach at age eleven, circa 1968.

Playing around with my fellow Buena Park Splashers, circa 1968.

My El Monte team, circa 1969: (*from left*) Cozette Wheeler, me, Coach Don Lamont, Kathy Calhoun, and Pam Reed.

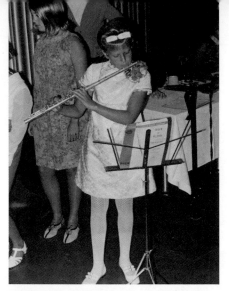

Playing the flute—my other childhood hobby—circa 1969.

Here I am (*far left*) getting ready to go on my first plane ride to Cincinnati for the Short Course Nationals in 1970.

CONGRATULATIONS!

You are now a member of the 1972 U.S. Olympic Swim Team.

This was how I found out I was going to the 1972 Olympics at the Trials in Chicago—a handwritten note waiting for me on the pool deck.

With my relay teammates—Sandy Neilson, Jane Barkman, and Jenny Kemp—at the 1972 Games in Munich.

With my puppy, Jerry, just after returning home from Munich in 1972.

Being honored in 1972 with Miss Orange County and some of my Olympic teammates: (*standing, left to right*) me, Susie Atwood, and Dana Schoenfield; and (*seated, left to right*) Keena Rothhammer and Sandy Neilson.

The letter I received from President Nixon after returning from Munich in 1972.

THE WHITE HOUSE
WASHINGTON

September 12, 1972

Dear Miss Babashoff:

All of America joins me in welcoming you home from the 1972 Summer Olympics. Your gold and two silver medals are splendid tributes not only to your skill as a swimmer but, perhaps more importantly, to your dedication to the ideals of the Olympic tradition. On behalf of your fellow citizens, I am delighted to extend my heartiest congratulations to you for the honor you have brought to yourself and to your country.

With my best wishes,

Sincerely,

Richard Nixon

At Disneyland in 1973 with backstroker Melissa Belote (*center*) and Aussie legend Shane Gould (*right*).

In my family's Fountain Valley backyard, circa 1974, with my three medals from the 1972 Olympic Games.

With Valerie Lee in Dallas for the 1974 AAU Championships.

Kelly Hamill and I just being '70s teenagers, circa 1975.

Publicity shots taken in Mission Viejo for programs at the various meets I swam in, 1975.

My little sister, Debbie, presenting me with a victory bouquet, circa 1975.

With my coach, the legendary Flip Darr, circa 1975.

WELCOMES U.S.A. NATIONAL SWIM TEAM • AUG. 25, 1975
TRAVEL ARRANGEMENTS BY CROWN TRAVEL COORDINATORS

Leaving for the World Championships in Cali, Colombia, 1975.

The official team photo for the World Championships in Cali, 1975.

Left: As the homecoming queen at Golden West College, 1975.
Right: With Kelly Hamill in Hawaii, 1975.

Making eyes at the great Don Schollander, circa 1976.

With my wonderful
coach, Mark Schubert,
in 1976.

Babashoff, Goodell
Shatter World Mark

Featured in an *L.A. Times* article with my coach, Mark Schubert, at the 1976 Olympic Trials in Long Beach.

Victory at the '76 Olympic Trials—one of the best performances of my life.

SWIMMING WORLD
AND JUNIOR SWIMMER

Vol. 17, No. 6/June 1976/$1.25

A *Swimming World* cover leading into the 1976 Montreal Games.

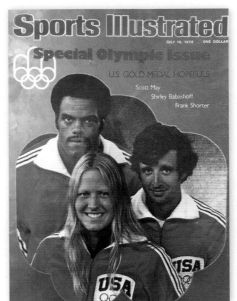

On the cover of *Sports Illustrated* with basketball player Scott May and long-distance runner Frank Shorter before the 1976 Olympics.

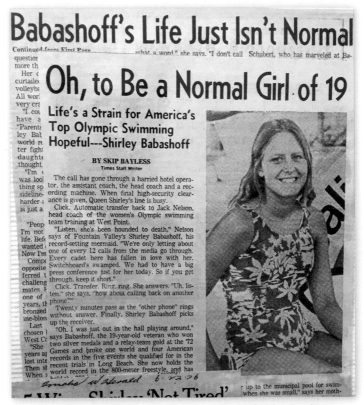

One of the first articles to refer to me as "Surly Shirley," written by columnist Skip Bayless and published in the *L.A. Times* in the summer of 1976, right before the Olympics began.

Meeting President Gerald Ford in Plattsburgh, right before we headed to Montreal for the '76 Games.

76 United States Olympic Women's Swimming Team

The official shot of the 1976 Olympic team. I'm in the back row, second from left.

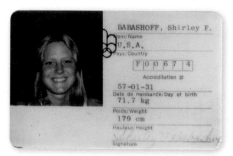

My official ID (*top*) and proof of sex for the 1976 Games.

Receiving one of my four silvers at the 1976 Games.

Being interviewed by Donna de Varona at the 1976 Games in Montreal.

East Germany's Petra Thümer (*left*) and Barbara Krause. According to reports, Krause was forced off the East German swimming team in 1976 because team doctors had miscalculated her dose of drugs and worried she might test positive at the Olympics.

Left to right: East German swimmers Kornelia Ender (who won four gold medals at Montreal in 1976), Ulrike Richter (who won three gold medals), and Birgit Treiber (who won one gold medal and two silver medals) in 1975. All were later proven to have been doping.

East Germany's Andrea Pollack won two gold medals and a pair of silvers at the 1976 Games at Montreal. In 1998, Pollack and her other teammates went public with accusations that they had been systematically doped by their coaches.

Hugging my teammate, Kim Peyton, just after we won the gold in the 4x100 freestyle relay at the 1976 Olympics in Montreal.

All smiles after winning the relay gold, 1976.

Taking our victory lap—trailed by the East Germans, oddly—after winning the relay gold, 1976.

Our victory lap with Old Glory, 1976.

With my teammates—Kim Peyton, Wendy Boglioli, and Jill Sterkel—on the victory stand after receiving our gold medals at the 1976 Games.

One of the most remarkable moments of my life—hearing the National Anthem after we won the relay gold in 1976.

Swimming

U.S. Women's Olympic Relay Swim Team

Our 1976 gold medal relay victory was used on a trading card.

AMATEUR ATHLETIC UNION OF THE UNITED STATES

UNITED STATES SWIMMING RECORD

This Is To Certify That

U.S.A. OLYMPIC TEAM
KIM PEYTON, WENDY BOGLIOLI, JILL STERKEL, SHIRLEY BABASHOFF

Established the following American Record

400 METER, 3:44.82 – 1976 WOMEN'S LONG COURSE FREESTYLE RELAY

and it was officially approved at the ____90th____ Annual Convention of the
Amateur Athletic Union of the United States.

CHAIRMAN, NATIONAL AAU
COMPETITIVE SWIMMING COMMITTEE

PRESIDENT
AMATEUR ATHLETIC UNION

The official certification for our 1976 relay win.

With Brian Goodell (*left*) and our coach, Mark Schubert, after the '76 Games.

Talking to reporters at the airport after the Olympics in Montreal.

Babashoff Retires

"I am just tired of swimming."

Shirley Babashoff
January 12, 1977

the swimmer...

the woman...

the winner...

The only American female swimmer who was able to keep up with the DDR the last four years, has retired.

Shirley Babashoff, the 20-year-old Olympic freestyle swimmer announced her retirement last month because, "I am just tired of swimming."

The UCLA co-ed was recently named American Female Swimmer of the Year for the third consecutive time after winning four silver medals and one gold in Montreal.

Babashoff currently holds three American records in the 200 meter free, 2:00.69, the 400 free, 4:10.46 and the 800 free, 8:37.59.

The Southern California native, set as many as six world records until the girls from the DDR got hold of her events. In 1972 Shirley knocked six-tenths of a second off the world record in the 200 free to gain the title with a time of 2:05.21. She later returned in 1974 to reclaim her title that had fallen twice since 1972, with a time of 2:02.94. One week later Shirley equalized her world record time again, in the 200 free.

In 1974 she set the world standard at 4:15.77 in the 400 free but came back a year later and broke her own world record with a time of 4:14.76. The record held for a whole year until Barbara Krause of the DDR cut three seconds off Shirley's time.

In 1976 Shirley held the world mark in the 800 free for four days until the present record holder, Petra Thummer, got in on the action by clipping Babashoff's time by two seconds.

A gold medalist in both Munich and Montreal Olympics for her part in the U.S. women's 400 meter freestyle relay, she was never able to win a gold in an individual event. She earned three silvers in Montreal in the 200, 400 and 800 freestyle. In 1972 at Munich she won two silvers in the 100 and 200 free.

the racer...

8

My retirement announcement in the January 1977 issue of *Swimming World*.

Signing with Arena in 1977 to become a spokeswoman for the brand.

Arena's Elite Team, 1977: (*front row, left to right*) David Wilkie, Don Schollander, me, Mark Spitz, and Gary Hall, as well as (*back row, left to right*) Steve Furniss, Micki King, Ulrika Knape, Klaus Dibiasi, and Novella Calligaris.

Playing with one of the photographers' lenses during a photo shoot in 1977.

SHIRLEY BABASHOFF

One of my publicity shots as a spokeswoman for Arena, 1977.

One of the things I liked about being a spokeswoman for Arena in 1978 was getting to speak with kids about swimming.

With my precious son, Adam, when he was about two years old, 1988.

Being photographed by *Sports Illustrated* in 1991 with Kornelia Ender and Adam.

Proof of East German Drug Use

By Phillip Whitten

There can no longer be any doubt about the reasons for the astonishing swimming success of East Germany's "wundermadschen."

Formerly secret documents "prove without a doubt that *every single East German world-class athlete* was doped," says Dr. Werner Franke, a distinguished German biochemist and a member of a national commission investigating the files of the Stasi, the East German secret police.

In a conversation with **Swimming World**, Dr. Franke described an all-encompassing system in which "clearance curves" were scientifically calculated to predict precisely when a steroid would clear an athlete's system and she or he would test negative.

Some of East Germany's greatest heroes, such as triple Olympic gold medalist Rica Reinisch, are now suing their sports medicine physicians and coaches, for the severe, permanent and life-threatening damage done by these drugs. Others, such as Christiane Knacke, the first woman to break a minute in the 100 Fly, have angrily denounced the system for using athletes as expendable guinea pigs.

It may have been unethical, but the East Germans were very good at their game: Despite *universal* use of illicit drugs, only one East German athlete *ever* tested positive at an international meet. *Swimming World* has obtained copies of the drug tests for Olympic great Kristin Otto and other top swimmers from the Stasi files. One document, published for

Kristin Otto

the first time anywhere, is reproduced here.

It shows that on August 9, 1989, Kristin Otto, Heike Friedrich, Daniela Hunger and Dagmar Hase all tested positive for anabolic steroids. The tests measured the ratio (Q) of testosterone (T) to epitestosterone (E).

According Dr. Robert Voy, M.D., former Chief Medical Officer for the USOC, a normal ratio is about 1:1, with men measuring slightly higher (up to about 1.2:1) and women slightly lower. Even in men with severe glandular disorders, ratios above 3:1 are rarely, if ever, seen. To avoid even the possibility of error, the IOC has proclaimed only ratios above **6:1** as indicating a positive test for steroids.

The tests on the East German swimmers show the following ratios:

Kristin Otto	**17.0:1**
Daniela Hunger	**12.5:1**
Dagmar Hase	**10.0:1**
Heike Friedrich	**8.8:1**

The letter reporting the test results was signed by Dr. Claus Clausnitzer, Director of the Central Doping Control Laboratory at the Central Sports Medical/Information Service in

Kresicha. The results had previously been given by phone to "Kolln Bismark" on August 8, 1989.

Coverage of the cheating East German team, published in *Swimming World* in 1994.

xxx

With my dear friend, John Naber, at the 2015 Golden Goggle Awards in Los Angeles.

With the great Michael Phelps at the Golden Goggle Awards.

Here I am in 2016.

great job! Wonderful performance!"?

After one of the races, an East German swimmer came over to me and said in broken English, in a very deep voice, "You need to shake our hands." Oh no I don't, I thought. I turned my back on her and walked the other way.

The great thing about having Mark in Montreal was how positive he remained, even as I kept coming in second place. He knew how to deal with me. He encouraged me and kept reinforcing the fact that I was swimming great times.

"Don't let them get you down, Shirley," he said. "You just keep doing your best."

Of course he was right, but it was easier said than done. Sometimes, when I wandered outside the Village and got mobbed by fans asking me to sign autographs, I wanted to ask them if they thought the East Germans were cheating. The fans were excited to be there, so I never asked. I didn't want to be a downer. But in the back of my mind, I wanted to say to them, "Look closely at what's going on. Something is not right here."

July 20 was the 400 freestyle. I had won the 400 free at the 1975 World Championships in Cali, Colombia. I'd also held the world record from 1975, until East Germany's Barbara Krause broke it by over three sets at a meet in Berlin, one month before the Games. But Krause would not be in Montreal; she had a throat infection and had been dropped from the East German team.

This seemingly left the race open for me, or so many thought. But once the race started, Krause's teammate, Petra Thümer (who had finished second behind me in my world record swim), took the lead and never let go. She opened with a half-second lead in the first 100 and maintained it throughout, eventually winning the gold medal in a world record time of 4:09.89. Right behind her, I also bettered Krause's record, finishing in 4:10.46, but it was only for the silver medal.

Pictures started appearing in newspapers all over the world of me up on the second-place podium, looking hurt, dejected, and worse. It's strange sometimes what a picture captures. In one of the photos, it looked as if I was wiping away a tear.

But I didn't feel hurt or sorrow up there. I was angry. I wanted to raise my hand in front of all those cameras and say, "Doesn't anybody care that they're cheating? How can they be allowed to do this over and over and over?"

At a certain point, I just hit a wall. Shirley, I told myself, there's nobody here to help you through this. There are no coaches or Olympic officials or international mediators or anyone that could step and do something about it. This is a done deal. This is just how it is. Deal with it.

I had a couple of days off until my next race, so I decided just to relax as much as possible. I struck out on my own a couple of times to walk the streets of Montreal, where occasionally I was recognized. Back in the Village, I hung out with my teammates and tried to focus on the next race: the 200 free. I had won this event at the 1975 World Championships, where Kornelia Ender had taken it out hard and died in the final 100 to allow me to pass her for the title. But in June of '76, Ender had become the first woman to swim 200 meters in under two minutes, breaking the world record in Berlin in 1:59.78.

On July 22, Ender let me take the lead for the first 100 meters, and then we were virtually even at 150. Then she really turned it on, finishing the final 50 in 28.88—almost as fast as her opening 50 of 28.63—and beating me with another world record of 1:59.26. Dutchwoman Enith Brigitha placed third, as she had in the 100 freestyle a few days before. Ender was on her way to a four-gold-medal Olympics, with one silver to boot.

I couldn't feel bad about my times. The 100 was my best time ever, the 200 was my second-best time, the 400 was my best time by a large margin, and our medley relay had gone really well. But the press kept pushing the story they had fabricated for me: that I had fallen short of my goals, so my performances could not be labeled a success. My mood increasingly got the better of me at all the post-race press conferences I was forced to attend, and every day, the media churned out stories about how "Surly Shirley" couldn't handle coming in second. Nobody was interested in digging deeper into what was going on. I was a much easier target.

I tried to contain my feelings, but it was hard. I was swimming some of the best times of my life, with no gold to show for it. I wasn't going to be a phony. I had no interest in backing off from what I knew to be true. I wasn't going to be part of everybody else's charade and behave as if the East Germans were actually earning their gold legitimately.

One more day left of the Games. Just one more day of competitions, and then it would all be over.

On July 25, I would be swimming in the 800, but the grand finale would be the 4x100 freestyle relay, which I'd be swimming with Jill Sterkel, Wendy Boglioli, and Kim Peyton. This was our last chance for glory. To most observers at the Games, fans and press alike, the assumption was that we basically had no chance. The East Germans, the darlings of Montreal, were the talk of the Olympics (though they did very little talking themselves; they made some perfunctory comments at press conferences and were then whisked out of the Village).

I really liked my relay teammates. They were all different, but each had her own charms. Kim was someone who was always laughing. If it wasn't funny, she would make a comment that was. She was always upbeat, no matter what. (And she left this world way too young. God, I miss her.) Wendy, the oldest of us all at twenty-one, was the most serious. She was super sweet, but not as goofy as the rest of us. Jill was the youngest and having the time of her life. Once she baked cookies for all of us in the Olympic Village kitchen and put way too much salt in them. Knowing Jill and her sense of humor, I knew better than to try them.

The night before the relay, we all felt like we needed some kind of plan. We had been getting our butts kicked all week, and it was time to do something about it. We decided that we weren't going to go down quietly. So me, Jill, and Kim (Wendy was with her family) gathered into our little apartment and put our heads together. Thus began one of the most memorable nights of my life. The three of us brainstormed about what we had to do to win the race.

We recalled that in Cali, our entire team had believed in the power of positive thinking before the races. This kind of thing was very popular in the 1970s, and while it had seemed silly to most of us on the team, we'd played along and read the literature they had given us and listened to the audiocassettes. It seemed harmless enough; it was just a basic program about how to be more productive and successful. These were some of the lessons we had learned:

1. Be a Team Player
To put it simply, roll with the punches. Part of being a team player is shouldering assignments or work that you do not find enjoyable, but that are necessary for the greater good of the team. The key is to recognize that greater good and your part in making it happen instead of focusing only on the inconvenience to you.

2. Avoid Complaining

Complaining is just about the biggest waste of time and energy out there. Every second spent complaining is a second that could have been spent improving. Besides, no one likes a complainer. If you have an issue, think of a solution before you bring it up in discussion. You will feel better for taking initiative, and others will be glad you didn't just turn to them for the solution.

3. Turn Problems Into Opportunities

When faced with a problem, take the "glass half full" approach. Problems are inevitable. So brace for impact and focus on the good that can come out of solving a problem—what you can learn by challenging the problem and how you can improve your life through its solution.

4. Focus on the Good, Not the Bad

It's easy to ignore the good and focus on the bad, because the good is what we want, whereas the bad sticks out more since it is unwanted. Try making a list of all that you enjoy about the situation at hand. Then consult this list on a regular basis to help remind yourself that the good typically far outweighs the bad.

It was pretty basic stuff, but all of the sudden, it felt like exactly what we needed to be thinking about in that moment. It had seemed silly before, but it now made sense to us. We had a foundation to work from, and we started to get motivated.

We started out by imagining what the race would be like, and even started acting it out. We laid down on the floor and visualized the race, imagining how fast we were going to swim, and what the transfers were going to be like during the relay. We mapped out and performed the race over and over and over in our heads. We described how we were going to swim to each other. We encouraged each other.

The more we talked it through, the more we started to feel like a real relay team. We discussed little things we could do to gain an edge. For me, a big part of this was how I was going to leave the block. The more I laid there, thinking about it, the more it hit me how much time most swimmers took waiting for the person before them to touch the wall. But why not start your take-off before they touched the wall? If you timed it just right, as their arm was coming down, you could gain a decent amount of time—as long as your toes didn't leave the deck before their fingernail hit.

We talked it out all night. To beat the East Germans, we were going to have to swim the best race of our lives. By the time we went to bed, we felt pretty confident. All of the stress and anxiety from the past week just kind of melted away. We had a good sense of what the East Germans' times would be, and what we would have to do to top them: swim flawlessly and execute our best performances together, as one.

The morning of July 25 came fast. The 800 free, which I'd be swimming in, was scheduled for the early evening; the 4×100 free relay would come after that. My teammates and I took it easy during the day. For fun, we went out and bought matching rainbow suspenders to wear when we walked into the arena later that night. It may sound kind of goofy today, but in our minds, it was an intimidation tactic: walking in looking unified, like a team. At that point, we were game for any advantage we could come up with.

The 800 was going to be a serious challenge. In 1974 and '75, the top distance swimmer in the world had been Australia's Jenny Turrell, who had won the 1975 World Championships in

Cali and set the 800 freestyle world record in London in March. She had also set five world records in the 1,500 freestyle, which was a non-Olympic event. But in June of 1976, East Germany's Petra Thümer had broken Turrell's 800 freestyle record with 8:40.68 in Berlin. Seventeen days later, I had bettered that mark. The three of us were expected to contest the medals in the 800 freestyle in Montreal, but Turrell had shoulder problems coming into the Olympics and was not as good as she had been in 1975.

In the 800 free, Thümer qualified the fastest, followed by my roommate at training camp, Nicole Kramer. I won heat three, closely trailed by Turrell. The final race was led by Canadian Shannon Smith through the first 300 meters, but then Thümer and I took over. We were in lanes 4 and 5 and it was super tight, just as it had been in the 400 five days earlier. The results were the same, too: Thümer won the gold in world record time (8:37.14) and I won the silver, also under the old world record mark. The bronze went to my teammate, Wendy Weinberg.

After the 800 free, we gathered together for the obligatory press conference.

"How do you feel having won only four silver medals so far?" one of the reporters asked me.

I turned to look directly at him. "How many silver medals have you won?" I asked. Then I got up and walked out of the room. At that point, I was all but done with the press. The truth was, I had just turned in my best time ever—two seconds under my old world record. That was something to be proud of.

There was just one race left, the final swimming event of the 1976 Games: the 4×100 free relay.

CHAPTER FOURTEEN

The Final Race

Before each race, after getting a pre-race rubdown, swimmers went down to the ready room, which was under the spectator stands. The room had a glass front, so the pool was visible. This was where they made sure all the competitors were present and ready to go, about twenty minutes before each race.

The ready room was a good place to sit and think one last time about your upcoming race. It was generally very quiet in there. That evening, my team gathered in the room and sat there together, remembering our positive-thinking exercises from the night before and thinking about what we needed to do in just a few minutes.

Our East German counterparts were sitting nearby, laughing and making out with their boyfriends, who were swimmers on the men's team. We stared at them, amazed. We wondered if they were trying to psych us out. If so, it wasn't working. To us, they just looked silly, and seemed almost disrespectful. We didn't let them get into our heads, though. We kept our mood light. We were loose, excited, and totally in sync with each other.

Suddenly, it was time to go out on the pool deck. When we stepped out onto the deck, we were met by a roar from the crowd. There were chants of "USA, USA," which made us feel good. The place was packed, and it seemed like everybody knew what was at stake.

My teammates and I got together one last time, looking each other in the eye and reminding each other about the night before. We knew we could do this. We knew we at least had a shot, even though I'm sure very few people there that night would have agreed with us.

Our team was in lane 3, with East Germany right next to us in lane 4. Sweden, the USSR, Canada, the Netherlands, France, and West Germany filled out the rest of the lanes. As the lead-off swimmers from each team lined up, things felt clearly tense. We waited for the gun, and then—a false start. I think everybody was a little bit on edge.

Everyone got back into place, and then *beep*—the gun went off, and the swimmers took off.

Leading off for our team was Kim, our country's fastest 100 swimmer with a best time of 56.81. Kornelia Ender led off the relay for the East German team. At these Games, Ender had already become the first woman to capture four gold medals in a single Olympics. She had set three world records, including the 100 freestyle (55.65).

After just twenty-five meters, Ender had powered out to nearly a body length's lead. This was going to be tougher than we had imagined. Watching Wendy get ready, I knew what she was thinking: *just stay close*. We had total faith that she could do that.

At twenty-one years old, Wendy was kind of like our "elder" on the U.S. national team. Swimming against her from East Germany was Petra Priemer, the Olympic silver medalist in the 100 free. Priemer maintained the lead, but Wendy stayed right within striking distance. The crowd around us was on its feet and roaring.

Next was Jill, who dove into the water a half body length behind East Germany's Andrea Pollack. At just fifteen years old, Jill had swum her best time (57.06) earlier in the competition, when she finished seventh in the 100. She stayed close to Pollack. On her second length, Jill turned on a thunderous kick that slowed her turnover rate and drove her to pull even with Pollack. Oh my god, I thought to myself. She's going to take the lead. It was incredible to watch. I took a big breath and exhaled. This was just what we wanted.

The crowd felt it, and the roar in the Natatorium was growing with the possibility of witnessing a tale akin to David defeating Goliath. Could it be? Did we really have a chance? A moment later, Jill passed Pollack. We had the lead! This was the moment. Natural talent was outperforming drug-enhanced.

Later, *Swimming World* would report:

> At the completion of 300 meters, Jill Sterkel touched in a stunning 55.78—the fastest split of all of the finalists. The Americans had the lead—by four-tenths of a second, 2:48.54 to 2:48.94—and broadcaster Donna de Varona screamed, "They have a chance!"

Standing on the deck, all of the relays I'd watched over the years were flashing through my head. When I'd seen those relays I'd always thought to myself, "Wow, they could have saved some time by a quicker leap off the deck." So, in that moment, I decided I was going to go for it. I was going to make the best jump of my life. The mother of all leaps. But I had to time it right. I wanted to be in the air as Jill touched the wall. I was poised and ready to explode, coiled like a cobra ready to strike.

As soon as Jill touched the deck, I leaped out into the air. It was the best jump of my life. But . . . had I left too early? In my zeal to execute the perfect start, I couldn't tell if it had been an *early* start—and I wouldn't find out until the end of the race. There was nothing to do now but swim.

I knew that all I had a do was protect our very short lead. With each stroke I took, I could hear the crowd growing louder and louder in my ears. East Germany's Claudia Hempel was right next to me, and I knew I still had the lead. I just kept swimming as hard as I could, feeding off of the roar of the now insane crowd.

Back then, I was one of the only swimmers to wear goggles. In fact, '76 was the first Olympics where goggles were worn. With my goggles on, I could sort of see where I was in relation to Hempel. But I had no idea if I was really winning. My only gauge was the growing roar of the crowd. With each stroke, I knew how close it was, so I pushed harder. The louder the crowd got, the harder I pushed.

Swimming World broke down the action beautifully:

With 85 meters remaining in the race and Hempel charging next to her, one question remained: Would Shirley let Claudia pass? Babashoff stroked madly, taking nearly 60 strokes per length, while Hempel powered through the water with greater efficiency. Shirley's muscles were tired from the effects of her 800 freestyle battle earlier that evening. With 40 meters remaining, Hempel raced at Shirley's shoulder. Babashoff's tempo increased even faster. While her muscles were weak, her resolve was like steel. Shirley Babashoff extended her fingertips to the touch pad, stopping the clock 68-hundredths of a second sooner than Claudia Hempel. She split 56.28 to Hempel's 56.56, and the American team smashed the GDR's world record by four full seconds!

When I touched the wall, I knew we had won but I quickly turned to look to the scoreboard and make sure there wasn't a little red light next to our team's name—that would've meant there was a disqualification. The place was going absolutely nuts. I jumped out of the pool and my three amazing team-mates and I hugged each other and screamed. We had done it. We'd done the impossible. At least, what the rest of the world had thought was impossible.

When Mark came down to the deck, I asked him if I had jumped too early. He told me I had done fine. One of the other countries challenged that I had left early, but after a quick in-spection of the videotape, it was ruled that everything was just fine. It had been close, but I had not left early.

As we gathered up our warm-up suits and made our way toward the medal podiums, people were screaming at us and cheering. They were ecstatic. A few moments later, when they played the national anthem and we stood on the podium with our gold medals around our necks, I had ever been more proud in my life. And I'll admit, I did turn my back on the East German girls when they came to congratulate us. I got a lot of criticism for that, and I understand why, but I stand by my protest. That was the last race of the Games, and even though we had some-how prevailed, it didn't change what had happened. I knew they were cheating. I didn't know how, but it was obvious to me. I simply could not accept their handshakes. I couldn't be phony.

When they played "The Star-Spangled Banner," something cool happened. The crowd cheered wildly *during* our national anthem. Of all the times I had stood on podiums after winning Olympic medals, I had never heard that happen. Then again, I'm not sure many crowds got to witness what had just occurred.

My three relay teammates and I exchanged looks and even giggled a couple of times at what we had just accomplished. We were giddy. Four American girls, in the limelight at last. We'd been all but totally written off at these Games. Nobody thought we could win—not the media, not the crowds, and certainly not any of the other athletes.

With our hands over our hearts, our hair still wet, and the

smell of chlorine heavy in the air, we savored the sound of the crowd that, moments before, had helped push us toward achieving what many had thought impossible.

I was so proud of my teammates standing next to me: Jill Sterkel, Kim Peyton, and Wendy Boglioli. This was everything we had ever dreamed of since swimming together as young girls on all of those teams, through all of those competitions. Looking at my relay teammates now, I realized that I didn't know what their plans were once we left Montreal, after we had packed our bags and gone back home to our regular lives. It was one thing to be traveling together and living together through all of the Trials, training, and then eventually the Games themselves. But we came from very different worlds. What would their life be like once they returned home? Sure, they would give speeches, attend luncheons, and receive keys to the city. There would be articles written and maybe even a small plaque placed by the pool where they swam as a child. But would they keep swimming? Where would their lives take them? I couldn't answer for them, but I knew how I felt.

All of the sudden, I sensed that I might be done. As monumental and exhilarating as it felt to be standing alongside my teammates with that gold medal around my neck, I no longer had faith in a system that seemed so corrupt. Everything that I had worked so hard for now felt like it had been for naught. I was exhausted physically, but also mentally. My spirit had been crushed, and I had started second-guessing myself.

After we received our medals, we paraded around the Olympic pool, holding up the American flag. Strangely, the East Germans took a victory lap with us. I had no idea what they were trying to prove, but I didn't care. We'd beaten them, fair and square. Nothing had changed. I still knew they were cheating, and I wasn't about to cut them any slack. But nothing was going to spoil our good time. We had done something very special, and the world was finally paying attention.

Years later, I asked my teammates, Wendy and Jill, to reflect on the race that day and their experience at the Games in general. Here's what Wendy said:

> *The 1976 relay with Shirley, Jill, and Kim was and remains a motivating and profound moment in my life. It was really my last chance at a medal. I was married, I was twenty-one years old, and I knew that was going to be my last Olympics.*
>
> *I was just so grateful to have made that team. I had barely missed making the '72 team, so this was a really big deal for me. I knew these Games were a big deal for Shirley, too. There was just so much pressure on her. Seeing the 100 freestyle on the first day, seeing Shirley finish where she did, along with how the rest of our teammates fared . . . well, that really set the tone for me. It was such an eye-opener watching my teammates finish as they did. We had prepared for those Games the best that we could. But the stakes changed once we arrived. And so, as well-prepared as we thought we had been, now we had to adjust quickly. I grew up swimming in lakes in Wisconsin. I didn't know about steroids or any of these mysterious drugs that were being talked about all of the sudden.*
>
> *My role on the team was sort of unique. I was a little bit older and I think I acted older, too, which made me seem even more mature. Because of that, some of the other girls called me "Mom" and I would do things like help get them to and from places on the bus and make sure they were always on time and things like that. I was just a few years older, but it felt like a lot more. Still, we had so much fun before getting to Montreal. The training at West Point was, for me, a great experience. Just before camp was over, we did a big swimming exhibition for the locals where they just*

opened the doors for free and everyone watched us perform, simulating relays and putting on a show. Then it was on to Canada, where the East Germans would soon be putting on a show of their own.

When I think of the relay, it is still mind-boggling to me that Shirley swam the 800-meter free right before that race. I mean, like twenty minutes before. I could never have done that, but she was just so strong. Freestyler Barbara Krause was not going to be swimming for the East Germans; she hadn't even made the trip because they said she'd become ill or something, which certainly worked in our favor but was by no means a lock for us to win. But we knew we had a shot. It was really based on how everyone swam that week that the order was set. Shirley and Kim and Jill got together the night before to discuss the race, but I spent that time with my mom and dad. Having them there, after all they had done for me in my life, was really important. But our coaches had talked to me about the relay and I knew what I had to do that next day. It was pretty basic: everyone had to swim their best times ever.

The morning of the race, the four of us all got together in the Olympic Village and decided we were going to wear suspenders, red pants, and matching T-shirts as a way of making a statement. We had nothing to lose and we were going to do things on our own terms. And have fun while we did it.

In the ready room, most of the other teams were pretty solemn, but we were cracking each other up laughing with each other and we got a lot of looks for that, but we didn't care. We were just letting off steam and staying loose. Two of our coaches, Jack Nelson and Frank Elm, sat with us again and explained to us what they felt we needed to do is, again, just swim our best times and definitely break the *fifty-five-second mark. We knew we wanted to give Shirley a lead. That was very important.*

I got to the pool early and took a nap behind the flags that were set up behind the medals podium. That was always part of my routine, a short nap before racing, and so that was at about 3:30 PM. They wanted us all there by 4:00, so I woke up around then once the others arrived. We went into the warm-up pool beforehand, which was nice. Everyone but Shirley, who still had that 800 to swim. But then she arrived, and as I said, we gathered in the ready room for that last huddle before hitting the pool deck.

Once we got out there, I was just so blown away by how calm and cool Kim was after the false start that had occurred. Such composure. Then the relay began, and watching Kim start off the way she did was like an out-of-body experience. She stayed as close as she could to Kornelia Ender in lane 4. We had lane 3. I was just so proud of her, and my pride grew as she came back. As I hit the water, I was feeling really good. My parents always told me growing up, "You were born to do this." And that's what I was saying to myself in my head. That was my rhythm as I swam: "You were born to do this, you were born to do this," over and over. I cut into the East German lead, swimming against Petra Priemer.

I got out of the water and watched in awe as Jill Sterkel overtook her person. We knew it was down to Shirley, and we knew she could do it. There was something so special about being with these women in this moment. The place was going crazy and you could tell, looking at Shirley, that she was ready for this moment. She got an incredibly strong jump, and then it was just a matter of holding the lead. The crowd grew louder and louder, and Shirley came home to us. When she touched ahead of East Germany, we just lost it. We screamed and jumped up and down and hugged each other. Nobody thought we could do this. Nobody had given us any real chance.

I'd had a lot of anger and frustration up until then about the East Germans, and I was vocal. They didn't even stay in the Olympic Village; they stayed on a boat in the harbor. They had no sense of camaraderie or anything, but as it turned out, I guess their coaches just didn't want them being studied too carefully by anyone. But it didn't matter. We had beaten them. We had won gold.

When I got home—me and my husband, Bernie, lived in a little apartment in New Jersey and I was going to college—I started getting death threats. The FBI started tapping our phone and our mail was monitored. It was unbelievable. All of the excitement and joy I had felt in Montreal was essentially gone after those things happened. The press accused us of sour grapes for picking on the poor little East German girls. It was awful. But people know the truth now. In my mind, the individual bronze I won is really a gold, because the East Germans came in first and second. So I can only imagine how Shirley feels. She had the most at stake, and it really cost her. But you can never take away what we did up there. That's forever.

These were Jill's memories of the relay and what it meant to her:

I was very young then, literally just fifteen years old. In certain ways, the '76 Games was just like another big meet for me. Your perspective at that age is just totally different. It's hard to really imagine the scope of where you are and just how big it is. You've swum big meets before and you know what it's like to be in front of a lot of people. And that's really what it was. It was a lot of people and a lot of excitement, and it was just totally cool to be there.

I remember getting ready for the relay. We had really started bonding at that point, leading up to that last race. A few days before, Shirley, Kim, and I went into the music room when you could play whatever albums you wanted. We put on a song by the Eagles, "Take It to the Limit," and started singing together, just belting it out. It was kind of a fun and crazy release for us, but that song became like a little theme. We were going to take it to the limit.

We sat up the night before and basically talked about what we had to do to win. I distinctly remember us all agreeing: if we want to win, we have to do these times. So we started to get an idea of what it would look like on paper. We just started getting it into our heads. This is what we have to do. It's not going to be easy, but it's not impossible either. When you start working it out like that, it starts to look real. All of the sudden, you can feel it. When you speak things out loud, you align to it.

And then the next day, we had another idea to kind of take a stand. We all wanted to dress the same, in suspenders and T-shirts. We needed sneakers, too, and back then there were guys from various shoe companies who were literally working out of their hotel rooms, selling shoes. Given what a big shot Shirley was, she got us in the door with the guy who was selling Pumas and that morning, we all got a pair of those to complete our outfit for later in the day.

When I watch the race today, it's totally different than what I remember. When you're swimming in a race like that, it's hard to process all that's going on at the time. But when you watch it today, you can really break it down to its parts. And it's so much fun to watch. Kim and Wendy were tremendous, then it was my turn. I remember flipping at the fifty and coming off the wall and seeing that, all of the sudden, I was pretty much even with the East German. I almost couldn't believe it. I was known for having good turns and I thought in this instance that I had had a pretty good one. But I didn't realize it was that good. In a couple of seconds, I actually had a lead. That's when I started my six-beat kick. Instinctively, I always went down the first length with a two-beat kick, and then used the six-beat on the way back. When I opened up that lead on her, in my head I was just telling myself, kick as hard and fast as you can. It was like my brain was talking directly to my feet. Just keep kicking, just keep kicking, as hard and as strong as you can.

I don't remember hearing the crowd at that moment. I just remember hearing the water, the intense splashing in those last twenty-five meters. And then it was up to Shirley. We were all watching her so intently, just cheering for her to keep that small lead. I remember when Shirley was just about ten or fifteen meters away from the wall on our side. The gap was closing between the two of them, but we all knew that Shirley was good to do it. And then when she touched the wall, we just went crazy. That's when I started hearing the crowd. That's when it got really emotional.

Up until the press conference after the relay, I really didn't understand much of what had been going on with Shirley. Being a few years younger, I didn't hang around with her that much, and fifteen is a lot different than nineteen. I was still pretty much the youngest person there, and I think a lot of things went over my head. I mean, there was a lot of talk and we all kind of felt as if we were up against this evil empire with the East Germans. I was pretty tough, so that didn't scare me. I was big and strong, and even though they may have been bigger and stronger, nobody was going to tell me I couldn't do something. But Shirley's situation, as I learned later in life, was really unique. She had so much *pressure on her and there were so many expectations, and then one by one, those things just got taken away from her.*

My first taste of what she was going through happened in the interview room right after the race. I was just so thrilled to be sitting in there, knowing that we had just won a gold medal. That's all I was thinking about. And then the very first question goes to Shirley and reporter asks, "So, Shirley, how does it feel to finally win a gold after getting four silver medals?" Shirley just stares the guy down and says, "Well, how many medals have you won?" And I thought to myself, wow, this just got real. You could feel the tension. I had no clue up until that point just how bad it was for her at those Games, but in that moment, it all became pretty clear. No matter what she did out there, people made it all about her and didn't even bat an eye at the East Germans. It was rough.

But we still felt the euphoria, late into the night. I remember thinking, wow, the races are all finished now, so we can do whatever we want. Kim and I wound up sitting on some church steps late that night, eating a bunch of doughnuts. That was our celebration. We just sat there with another friend from our team, Rick Colella, I believe, and that was how we celebrated.

I'll never understand cheaters. I kind of lost faith in the system once I learned everything that was going on up there, because once people are cheating, the essence of the Games is gone. There's no longer a level playing field. And the whole point of competition is that everybody plays by the same rules. When you take that away, the Games don't really mean that much. But nobody knew was happening back then, and given what we know today, I actually think that our gold medal means a lot more. We did what nobody thought we could do, and we did it the right way.

Back in my room that night after the race, I couldn't stop staring at my gold medal. In that very same room just twenty-four
hours earlier, my teammates and I had decided we were going
to win. And then we went out and did it. No matter what else
happened, they couldn't take this away from us. Lying in bed, I
replayed the relay over and over in my mind. It was wonderful.
I slept very well that night.

Now that the swimming portion of the Games was over,
we had almost a full week to spend in Montreal just watching
events or sightseeing or doing whatever we wanted. With the
pressure of the competition behind me, I was now more aware
of the reaction to the comments I'd made earlier in the week.
Everybody was thrilled about our win in the relay, but the media still managed to focus on me and why I wasn't behaving the
way they wanted me to.

That week, I had a strange dream. I was about to swim a
relay race in a big indoor pool when a fog suddenly rolled in.
The girls swimming ahead of me stopped halfway across the
pool, before they reached the fog, and then turned around and
swam back to the start. They did their turns right in the middle
of the pool, and I couldn't tell if they were cheating when they
swam back.

I mentioned the dream to a female reporter one day. Her
eyes opened wide and she said, "You think you were dreaming
about what it would be like to cheat sometime in your life?"

Reporters had a habit of saying the stupidest things to me.
I hate to be blunt about it, but that was just my experience. I
hadn't had the best experience with the media, to put it mild-
ly. I mean, this was just two years after Watergate; you would
think that, somewhere in the sea of reporters covering the
Games, there might have been a journalist who was interested

in investigating the East German women's team a little more closely. It could have been the story of the century, a Pulitzer Prize waiting to happen. It was staring everyone in the face, but nobody wanted to touch it. The "vaccine," it seemed, would remain a mystery.

CHAPTER FIFTEEN

A National Disgrace

A couple of years earlier, I had been in Australia for about a week and a half during the Australian Nationals, and I'd met a guy there named Graham Windeatt. He was this really cute long-distance swimmer from down under, and I had developed a bit of a crush on him. How could you not? He was good-looking and had that marvelous Australian accent. I wish I hadn't been so shy at that time.

Graham and I had gotten along really well, and one day he drove me up the coast to a lifeguard competition in his little Aston Martin. Nothing happened between us, but it was still kind of a magical day. Up until that time in my life, I'd really had no time for boys, and when you're traveling to somewhere exotic like Australia and you meet somebody like that, there's something very romantic about it. Especially to a seventeen-year-old girl.

Whenever I swam anywhere, in any competition, I wondered if Graham was going to be there. But I knew for sure that he would be at the Montreal Games, as the captain of the Australian men's swimming team. After I swam my last race, we ran into each other and hung out together for the final few days of the Olympics. It was wonderful. I remember sitting with him and listening to the new Frampton *Come Alive* album, which we both loved. I had a serious crush on him. I could sense that the Australian girls' swimming team was overly protective of him, and they could get pretty nasty if anyone from the outside got too close to him. ·

The Games had become so miserable for me in so many ways, despite the triumphant victory at the end. I wasn't sure I could go on anymore as a competitive swimmer, not after being cheated like that. So, to be able to spend time with this handsome and thoughtful young man was just what I needed. He was shocked to learn that I had been carrying this crush around. But that's how both our lives were. We traveled endlessly around the world and occasionally slowed down to lead normal lives and make sense of our feelings. I was in Graham's room when he was packing, the night before he left, and he kissed me. That's all that happened in his room. We wrote letters after we both got home, but eventually we went back to our own worlds and that was the end of it.

Right before the closing ceremonies in Montreal, the sports journalist Joe Gergen wrote a column in *Newsday* that still makes me angry to this day.

He began:

They are young, tall, and vigorous, with suntanned skin and bleached hair. They are superior athletes who have enjoyed considerable success in the past and appear unable to cope with the slightest hint of failure.

In my opinion, he had zero clue about what was really happening there.

They are the spoiled youngsters who comprise the United States women's swimming team, and they are the ugly Americans of the 1976 Olympic Games. Forget what they have done in the competition. Second place is nothing of which to be ashamed. Rather, it is what they have said which has been a source of dishonor both to themselves and their country. "Surly" Shirley Babashoff and her teammates have mocked the team of East Germany which defeated them, and in the process mocked the Olympic spirit.

No, we did not. If Mr. Gergen had done his job as a reporter, he would've discovered the truth behind what I had been speaking out about. This is where all the journalists could have done the country a favor by actually investigating the East German women.

If the U.S. women do not want to lift weights and enter heavy training, that is their privilege.

Enter heavy training? Was he even aware that I had been swimming twenty miles a day for four years? And training with weights for eight years?

So when the U.S. women raise the femininity issue as the reason why they failed to defeat the East Germans, it is not only insulting, but misleading. Apparently, the Americans can't decide whether they want to be treated as princesses or athletes. Clearly the East Germans have chosen the latter, which is an outgrowth of their ideology and culture, and that is not something to be derided by leering, snickering innuendos from a group of adolescents who suffer from tunnel vision.

Sorry, Mr. Gergen, I will never respect cheating. I will never respect systematic programs that destroy the lives of young women. Again, you could've done your homework. But you didn't. Very few in the media did. But to this day, Mr. Gergen stands tough by his position and still sees us all as a bunch of spoiled brats. I'd love to ask him: What if you worked for four years and then didn't get paid? Would that have been all right?

The closing ceremonies at Montreal were bittersweet for me. I was excited that we had won the relay, but of course I was still angry about the East Germans. I really appreciated that my friend, John Naber, helped make the day more fun for me. Understanding what I'd gone through, he went out of his way to walk side-by-side with me around the track that day, waving and smiling at people who were calling out our names. He wasn't going to let me feel down that day. John's nature is just so sweet and fun that he makes everything better. I was just so proud of him. He had won four gold medals and set a world record in each of those victories. The following year, he would be awarded the James E. Sullivan Award, presented to the top amateur athlete of the year.

My friend Brian Goodell swam wonderfully, too. He won two gold medals in the 400-meter and 1,500-meter freestyle events. The next year, *Swimming World* would honor him as the Male World Swimmer of the Year. Our American guys were just amazing. Even my brother, Jack, won a silver medal in the 100-meter freestyle. I hardly saw him at all during the Games, but I was proud that he had medaled.

In the end, the United States finished with thirty-four gold medals, thirty-five silver, and twenty-five bronze, for a total of ninety-four medals. Russia led with a count of forty-nine gold, thirty-one silver, and twenty-five bronze, and East Germany produced forty gold, twenty-five silver, and twenty-five bronze.

The East German women's team won gold medals in eleven

of the thirteen swimming events. In terms of gold, had they not cheated, I would have been the most decorated female swimmer in Olympic history.

When our plane landed back home at LAX Airport, our parents and some of the Mission Viejo swimmers were there to welcome us home—and a few reporters, of course. Everybody was cheering and happy, and I tried to look like I was, too. But inside, I was angry and mentally exhausted. All those hours in the pool, all those miles of swimming, just to lose to people who were obviously cheating. It was the event that could have changed my life forever, and it was all stolen right out from under me, in front of the whole world. I was heartbroken.

I heard rumors after we got home that some of my teammates had started getting not just hate mail, but letters with actual threats. There was this attitude out there that we had embarrassed our country. I was the only one who had spoken out, but some people were blaming our entire team. As far as threatening notes to me, I was never aware of them, but I think my mom was running interference on my mail and destroying hate mail that I received.

After the Olympics, the media treated me like trash. Despite the fact that we had just won a gold medal in one of the most exciting races in history, they chose to focus on the negative. *Time* ran a photo of me with a single word in the caption: "Loser." Reporters either accused me outright of being a sore loser, or they prodded me in an attempt to get me to admit how angry I was. But I didn't cave. I didn't want to give the East Germans the satisfaction of knowing just how upset I was.

My teammates and I were being attacked by our own country.

Our coaches at the Games did not speak out on my behalf. They let me take all the grief. I was convinced that Jack Nelson was there for himself; there was no way he would've stuck is neck out for me.

Surprisingly, my mother was my biggest defender. To counter all of the negativity against me, she wrote a letter to the *Los Angeles Times* that they published:

August 21, 1976

"MATERNAL VIEW OF BABASHOFF"

*I would like to show you a different side of Shirley Ba-
bashoff. The girl I know has gotten up at 4:45 AM for the
last four years. She has to drive for thirty minutes to work
out and thirty minutes home twice a day. She has given up
many of the social affairs that come with being a teenager in our country. She's a girl who was put in five hours a
day training in a sport she loves, for a country she wouldn't
trade for anything. At nineteen, not many girls would be
willing to come home at 12 from a party because of a training program.*

*Shirley has already trained for ten years but her last
four years have been the hardest, and she has never gotten a penny. She has been criticized by the press as being a
snob, but the press is not all roses either. These kids are not
trained for the tricky questions presented to them by many
reporters. They have stories written about them by reporters
warranted at the Olympics who haven't even talked to them.
Then you read an article that said Kornelia Ender said she
was happy with the silver and someone said, that's class. Yet
when Shirley used those same words, she was criticized.*

*Today we went to Disneyland and I saw at least thir-
ty people stop her for pictures and autographs, which she*

posed for and signed, always with a smile. This is just a part
of the story of Shirley Babashoff, who won four silver med-
als and one gold and did badly at the Olympics.

Mrs. Babashoff, mother of Shirley Babashoff

I appreciated that my mother did this. For all of her faults, her letter to the editor showed a flash of maternal responsibility; a mother defending one of her cubs. What prompted or inspired it? I don't know. Was it genuine? I hoped so. Or was it just another attempt to try and create some sense of public normalcy to help hide our severe dysfunction? I will never know for sure. But I was happy that she wrote it. I guess there was still a little girl inside of me who wanted to be protected and cared for by her mom.

I didn't speak to my teammates after I got home, but I wondered if they felt as underappreciated as I did. What was all that work even for? We had just been swept under the carpet. If that's where people want me, I thought to myself, that's where I'll stay.

It was time to acclimate to my new life. No more pre-dawn practices or late night training sessions. Thanks to some scholarship money I'd earned from swimming, I decided to go to UCLA. It was close to home, and I could come back on the weekends to babysit my sister, who was six years old at the time.

I considered swimming on the women's team at UCLA. I went to the first practice to check it out, and the coach told the swimmers we were going to do weightlifting with the program designed by the female arm-wrestling champion of the world. I didn't get what arm-wrestling and swimming had to do with each other, but I decided to give it try.

But when the arm-wrestling champion walked in, I immediately started having flashbacks of the East Germans. She was huge. She looked like Arnold Schwarzenegger with a woman's head. I knew right away that this was not going to be good. She wanted us to lift the heaviest weight possible for us and do ten reps. It was so hot in the weight room that people were passing out. This woman would yell at us in a husky voice for not trying hard enough, with spittle spraying from her mouth. She was like a drill sergeant.

When we got into the pool after the weight room, we were completely useless. Nothing would work. Our arms and legs felt like jelly. It was not fun. In fact, it was fairly miserable, all of it. So I left the team. It just wasn't for me.

In December, I was invited to ride in the famous Tournament of Roses Parade. That cheered me up. I had already been in a bunch of parades over the years—local parades in Fountain Valley and other nearby cities, and a couple of Disneyland parades. So on New Year's Day in 1977, I rode on the very last float in the parade, which was sponsored by Honda. I remember as we turned one corner, all of my friends were there in the crowd, screaming and waving at me. Honda also gave me an orange Honda Express motorcycle, which I was ecstatic about.

It was also the start of a very important month in my life. I had a decision to make, and it was a big one. The next Olympic Games were to be held in Russia in 1980. Everybody wanted to know: Was I preparing for those Games?

I thought a lot about what had happened in Montreal and the four years before that, when I had been swimming twenty miles a day. The more I considered my options, the more frustrated I became. Did I really want to commit myself to swimming that long and hard in training, only to go through another experience where I would feel cheated? It was still so fresh in my mind—that sickening feeling of having worked so hard every day, only to have somebody else reap the rewards. Did I want to do that again?

If the International Olympic Committee had been planning on investigating the East German women's swimming team's wins, my decision would have been easy. But there was no hint of that. At that point, everyone was celebrating the East German women's swimming team, and nobody was challenging their wins. All the talk about the American team after the Olympics had been focused on what a poor sport everyone thought I was. "Surly Shirley." I certainly wasn't about to start criticizing the East Germans again; I didn't want to have to endure the attacks all over again.

The thought of not swimming anymore as an amateur was tough to stomach. Ever since I was a little girl, everyone had known me as an amateur swimmer. It had been my whole life. But now, I also had to think about my future.

"I'm just not sure I can do this anymore," I told Mark over the phone. "I really have no complaints. I got to travel a lot, I met a lot of great friends, and I'm proud of how I got this one for my country. But after the last four years, I just can't imagine working that hard only to get screwed over again the way I was."

Mark understood completely. "You have nothing to be ashamed of," he said. "It was terrible what happened to you up there, and I wish more can be done right now. But until people start putting together some actual hard proof, it's going to be tough. Nobody ever worked as hard as you, and the standards you set for our club will make a difference for a long time. Don't ever think you're not appreciated, because you are. It's been an absolute pleasure coaching you."

With all of that in mind, I made the decision to retire from amateur swimming.

I didn't make a huge deal about it, but word got around quickly. The press found out immediately, and within a day or two there were plenty of headlines. UPI ran this piece:

America's Best Female Swimmer
Shirley Babashoff Calling It Quits

Shirley Babashoff, America's premier woman swimmer, is hanging up her racing suit.

The twenty-year-old swimmer, whose eleven-year career netted her eight Olympic medals and trips to dozens of foreign countries, announced Thursday she is retiring from competition.

The retirement will be complete. Babashoff, whose forte was freestyle, says she will not even try out for the women's swim team at UCLA, where she is a junior majoring in business.

"Basically, it was a correct decision on her part," said Mark Schubert, Babashoff's longtime coach. "She has been on top longer than any other female swimmer in the last five years. Now she wants to concentrate on other things— her studies at UCLA and perhaps a business career."

The other stories and headlines said basically the same thing. I never mentioned the emotional impact that Montreal had had on me. I just wanted to keep things low-key and slip away quietly. If I had even mentioned the word Montreal or referred to the East Germans at all, the attacks from the press would have started again. I didn't want to go there anymore. I was tired. I was drained.

I needed some time in my life to figure out what was next. It was going to be a whole new world for me, not practicing every day and building a life outside of swimming—at least, swimming competitively, as I had done for so long. I knew I still wanted to be involved somehow. Maybe I could coach or give lessons—anything that would keep me near the water, which I still loved.

One night, a few days after I announced my retirement, I was at home watching television in the living room. I flipped through the channels and stopped when an episode of *Charlie's Angels* came on the screen. In one scene shot near a swimming pool, Kelly, played by Jaclyn Smith, pulled back her white terry cloth robe to reveal a bikini she was wearing underneath. As she stood there posing, Jill, played by Farrah Fawcett, said to her, "Shirley Babashoff, eat your heart out!"

It was weird hearing my name referenced on a big television show like that, especially right after I had retired. Swimming was huge at the time, so much so that the writers of *Charlie's Angels* obviously had no doubt that viewers would know who Farrah was talking about. It made me a little sad to think that, now that I was retired, things like this would eventually stop happening.

After my retirement, I accepted an offer to appear on the ABC television show *The Superstars*, which pitted elite athletes from different sports against each other in a sort of decathlon-style competition. The catch was that you could not compete in your own sport. I flew down to Florida for the taping and competed in a variety of events from bowling to basketball and won a few thousand dollars. It was fun, and some of the other competitors included the figure skater JoJo Starbuck and Janet Guthrie, the race car driver.

A week or two after taping *The Superstars*, I received offers from both Speedo and Arena to become a spokesperson for their brand. I had always been a Speedo girl when it came to choosing my suits, but Arena offered a bit more money and that mattered to me. It wasn't a fortune—certainly nothing like what I would have been offered if I'd won five or six gold medals at the Olympics—but it was a nice offer and even allowed me to put a down payment on a small house in nearby Westminster.

The Arena brand was created by sports visionary Horst Das-sler, son of the Adidas founder and president of Adidas France. During the Munich Games, Dassler had been on the pool deck when Mark Spitz won his historic seven gold medals. Dassler, along with the rest of the world, had found himself in awe of Spitz, not only because he was the first athlete to win seven golds in one Olympiad, but also because he had set seven new world records in doing so. Dassler immediately started forming plans for a swimwear company dedicated to aquatic sports and created the new performance swimwear brand known today as Arena.

I was excited to work with Arena. I signed a contract with them to do personal appearances and allow them use my name and likeness in their advertising. They were putting together a "Team Arena" for a marketing campaign, made up of swim-mers and divers from all around the world. Forming Arena's Elite Team were me, Mark Spitz, Steve Furniss, Gary Hall, Don Schollander, and Maxine "Micki" King of the United States, David Wilkie of the United Kingdom, Ulrika Knape of Sweden, and Novella Calligaris and Klaus Dibiasi of Italy.

With this contract, I would have to work no more than fif-ty-six days each year for four years. I decided to stop going to school; I had never been happy there, and I had been struggling to make good grades. College wasn't for me.

Working for Arena was good for my self-confidence. All I did was promotional work, but it was fun. I started traveling again, which I had really missed. It was amazing to visit the Arena home office in France. The company took all of us athletes to a beautiful hunting lodge where we lived like kings for several days. We traveled to Japan a couple of times, and the Japanese people were lovely as usual and very respectful. I felt like they gave me the respect I hadn't gotten from my own country.

One of the most memorable trips was a hilarious appearance I did with Mark Spitz at a sporting goods store in Billings, Montana. We flew into Billings on a tiny twin-engine plane. The plan was to spend the day signing autographs in the store. But, as you can imagine, there weren't a lot of swimming fans in Billings, especially during the winter. Instead, Mark and I spent most of the day answering questions from hunters about where things were located in the store, or what kind of ammo they should buy. They had no idea who we were.

Mark was very sweet to me during the Arena years. Often when we'd arrive at LAX to check in for our flights, the agents at the desks would coo, "Oh my, Mark Spitz! We'd like to upgrade you to first class!" He was a rock star. But he would always insist that they upgrade me, too.

That first year after the Olympics was brutal on my ego and my psyche, but working for Arena helped me find my identity again and affirmed that I still mattered as an athlete. My memories of the Games haunted me, but I had worked through a lot of my anger toward the East Germans.

Working for Arena was almost like a lifeline for me. It allowed me to put a swimsuit on and go talk to people, especially kids, and tell them what it felt like to be a champion swimmer.

CHAPTER SIXTEEN

Marriage

About a year into my Arena contract, I met a sweet guy named Fred at a funeral for someone in our church, and we started dating. He was an agriculture student at San Luis Obispo in central California. He proposed to me and, within a few months, we were married. Our wedding was a very traditional Russian ceremony featuring borscht, lots of beef, tea, and the singing of prayers.

Unfortunately, Fred was only sweet up until the second we got married. Almost immediately afterward, he turned into a very possessive person, kind of a Dr. Jekyll and Mr. Hyde situation. One day during our honeymoon, he brought home some mussels to use as bait on a fishing trip. I grabbed a knife and started opening the shells for him. He suddenly went crazy, yelling at me, "That's the wrong knife, you stupid bitch! What do you think you're doing?" Right then, I knew something was very wrong. That was the beginning of the end right there, during our honeymoon.

Fred soon got a job in Fresno. For me, it wasn't exactly the most desirable spot in California, but I was going to try and make it work. All I really had going for me at that point was my Arena contract, but that hardly took any time out of the year. So, with nothing better to do, I just decided to be a good wife to this guy. That decision turned out to be a big mistake.

One day, Fred and I rode out to the dump in his truck to get rid of some garbage. As we unloaded the trash out of his flatbed out there in the middle of nowhere among the dry agricultural fields and horse farms, he looked at me and said, "You know, I could kill you out here and nobody would ever know that your body was here." This was maybe six months after we were married.

I didn't know what to do. I felt stuck with him, out there in the middle of nowhere. Sometimes, he would look at me and say, "You're like my little gold mine." It finally hit me one day—he felt like he had married some rich and famous celebrity swimmer who had tons of money flowing in for the rest of her life. I don't think he really understood who I was or what I was about. We had really just gotten married out of convenience, because of all the subtle pressure that families in the Russian church put on you, coupled with the fact that I didn't really have a plan for my life at that point.

Things just kept getting worse. One time in the kitchen, I said something he didn't like and he came over to me, grabbed my breasts, and twisted my nipples so hard that I could've started crying. I called my mother and spoke to the preachers who had married us to ask if they knew anything else about this guy. They told me, "Oh yeah, he's always been like this, very physical and he attacks people." It would have been nice if someone had given me a heads-up.

Fred took a new job near Bakersfield, so we moved again, to another city in the middle of nowhere. Just agriculture and horse farms. Fred started poisoning the ground squirrels in our yard so they wouldn't eat the fruit off of the trees, but in doing so, he killed three of our dogs in just two months. It was just horrible. A living nightmare.

In 1978, I was invited to compete again on the TV show

The Superstars, and this time it would be taped in the Bahamas. Fred came along on the trip and pretty much ruined everything. He was angry that I wasn't winning a lot of money, and kept accusing me of "goofing off" and screamed at me wherever we went. He had started hitting me at that point, too. I heard more stories about what he'd been like when he was younger, and the things he'd done to people.

One day, Fred actually struck me with a stick. That's when I decided to leave. I'd had enough. I packed up quietly and headed back home to my parents' house in Fountain Valley. I left Fred a note saying that this was it, and I couldn't take it anymore.

One of the first things I did when I got back home was paint my fingernails. Strangely, Fred hadn't let me do this. He had told me that only streetwalkers painted their nails, and I think he would've killed me if I'd done it while living with him.

A day or two after I arrived back in Fountain Valley, there was a knock at the door. Through the screen, I could see Fred standing there. When I answered the door, he apologized profusely and begged for my forgiveness. He seemed meek and contrite, until he caught a glimpse of my freshly painted nails. He gave me a disgusted look and said, "I knew you painted your nails." And with that, he left. I didn't see him again, and that was the end of my marriage.

Growing up, I'd never had a positive male role model at home, so I honestly had no clue what to expect from a husband. But it didn't matter. Fred was bad news. Maybe I should have been smarter when I first met him, and looked for red flags. But then again, maybe I just didn't know what to look for.

Working just fifty-six days a year left a lot of free time on my hands. My coach from the Golden West College men's swimming team, Tom Hermstad, suggested that I teach swimming. He ran a summer program at McGaugh Elementary School in Seal Beach, a small, laid-back beach town nearby. I loved it there and thought it would be a great place to work every day.

In order to teach at McGaugh, I had to become certified. I took a class on how to teach people to swim, and became a Red Cross-certified teacher. I had never thought about how hard teaching can be. A lot of people hate getting their faces wet, some have had bad experiences as children, and others are just really uncomfortable being in the water. Despite all of that, the most important factor, Herm told me, was to make sure it was fun.

Teaching was so gratifying for me that I continued to do it for the next several years. My oldest pupil, who was eighty-six years old, told me that she had dreamed of buying a boat ever since she was a child, and she planned on making that dream a reality as soon as she learned how to swim. I had her doing laps in just ten days, and then she got her boat. Teaching was so rewarding, but it was hard to make a good living from it.

In late 1979, I took a job starring as myself in a commercial for cotton towels. In February the next year, I was watching the Winter Olympics on TV with a bunch of friends when my commercial came on. It showed me swimming at the University of California in Irvine and then in a pool at a beautiful Beverly Hills mansion. The ad showed me using cotton towels at both the college and my glamorous mansion. The announcer said, "Medalist Shirley Babashoff. In the pool or out, performance and comfort just plain go together." Then I looked at the camera and said my big line: "That's why my towels are one hundred percent cotton. Super absorbent, super soft, and super comfortable. 'Cause they're cotton."

My friends were freaking out. "You're famous!" one of my girlfriends yelled. Well, I thought, maybe not *famous*. But it was fun seeing myself on TV, swimming in a beautiful pool. To me, it looked like a fantasy of what could have been.

That was the night of the famous Miracle on Ice game, the most exciting game in Olympic hockey history. It was amazing to watch Team USA beat Russia. My friends and I were going wild. After the win, some of my friends asked me if I could relate to the U.S. hockey players' fight against the Russians, since Team USA had been considered the underdogs. I guess I could, in a way. But I had never considered my team to be the underdogs at the Olympics in '76. In my mind, we had been the best. Watching the hockey game, I had no doubt that both the Russian and U.S. teams were exceptionally well-conditioned and talented. Team USA just outplayed them. Our swimming team's situation had been different. But I did understand that the hockey game probably felt a lot like our race had four years earlier, just in terms of the excitement and unexpected nature of it.

I felt so good for those guys on TV. I knew what it felt like to achieve something really special at the Olympics. When it happened, you knew you were a part of history in that moment.

That year, the United States did not participate in the Summer Olympics. Our government—as well as Japan, West Germany, China, Argentina, Canada, and the Philippines, among others—had decided to protest the Games because they were being held in the Soviet Union, which had invaded Afghanistan. As a result of the boycott, the Liberty Bell Classic, aka the "Olympic Boycott Games" were held in Philadelphia, featuring the countries that were participating in the protest.

Even though the U.S. wasn't competing in the official Games, I was curious to see how the East German women's swimming team would perform. Without the Americans there to challenge them, I thought, they would probably do pretty well. Sure enough, they were more dominant than ever. In the 100-meter, 200-meter, and 400-meter freestyle events, the

East German women took the gold, silver, and bronze. Same thing in the 200-meter backstroke and the 100-meter butterfly. Overall, East Germany came in second to the Soviet Union in total medal count, winning forty-seven gold, thirty-seven silver, and forty-two bronze.

Of course, nobody said anything about it. God only knows what East Germany was doing at the Games, but nobody was talking about it. The East Germans had simply established themselves as the new swimming powerhouses, and they were going completely unchallenged by the media. Nobody was speaking out. Nobody was calling them on the carpet. It would've been funny if it weren't so sad.

With my Arena contract finished, the early 1980s were fairly quiet for me. I had plenty of time on my hands, so I started teaching and coaching some local swim teams and just enjoying my new, simple life, trying to figure out what I would do next. I had my own small house in Westminster, just one city over from my parents in Fountain Valley.

In 1982, I was inducted into the International Swimming Hall of Fame in Fort Lauderdale, Florida. A plaque was unveiled, and they had lots of pictures from my career on display. That was truly an honor. I even got to put my handprints in wet cement. This was what they wrote about me for the induction:

SHIRLEY BABASHOFF (USA)
1982 HONOR SWIMMER

FOR THE RECORD: OLYMPIC GAMES: 1972 gold (relay), silver (100m, 200m freestyle); 1976 gold (relay), silver (200m, 400m, 800m freestyle; relay); WORLD RECORDS: 11 (200m, 400m, 800m freestyle; 5 relays); AAU

NATIONALS: 27 (100m, 200m, 400m freestyle; 11 relays); WORLD CHAMPIONSHIPS: 1973 gold (200m, 400m freestyle), silver (2 relays); 1975 gold (200m, 400m freestyle), silver (2 relays), bronze (800m freestyle); AMERICAN RECORDS: 39 (100m, 200m, 400m 500m, 800m freestyle; 22 relays).

One of the great women freestylers of all time is Shirley Babashoff. During her eleven-year swimming career, mostly with the Mission Viejo Nadadores, Shirley was 1974 U.S.A. Sportswoman of the Year, Swimming World Magazine's American Swimmer of the Year for 1976, and a thirty-nine-time American Record holder. Her greatest meet was the 1976 Olympic Trials in which she won all freestyle events and the 400 I.M., while setting three American records in the prelims, three more in the finals, and a world record in the 800 freestyle finals. Her Olympic and World Championship achievements were only slightly less spectacular. In the Olympics, she won two silvers and a relay gold in 1972 and followed this with four frustrating silvers and anchoring the gold medal freestyle relay in 1976. In the World Championships at Belgrade and Cali, she won two golds, seven silvers, and a bronze. This hard-swimming iron woman also won twenty-seven U.S. AAU Nationals, set eleven World Records, and was high point winner five times in the U.S. Nationals.

It was nice to be acknowledged for what I had accomplished as a swimmer. It sparked my interest in the swimming world again.

CHAPTER SEVENTEEN

The Charade Continues

Whenever the Olympics rolled around, it always caught my attention when athletes were busted for doping. Back in 1976, the weightlifters had been the ones who often got caught, including a couple from the United States. It was almost always for anabolic steroids. At the 1984 Games in Los Angeles, a wrestler and a couple of Japanese volleyball players were busted along with the weightlifters. Still, nothing that could be described as a "state-sponsored program." I attended a couple of the events in Los Angeles as a spectator, and was part of a parade (along with Buster Crabbe) at Disneyland.

East Germany was noticeably absent from the 1984 Games. As payback for the U.S.-led boycott of the 1980 Summer Olympics in Moscow, fourteen Eastern Bloc countries and allies, led by the Soviet Union, initiated their own boycott several months before the 1984 Games began. Much like the alternate "Olympics" held in Philadelphia back in 1980, the Eastern Bloc countries created an event called the Friendship Games, held in the Soviet Union. Guess which team won the most gold medals in swimming? Why, East Germany, of course, taking sixteen gold to the Soviet Union's thirteen. The East Germans continued to shatter world records, too.

Being out of the world of professional swimming, I no

longer had a platform from which to voice my opinions about the East Germans. But more and more, I lost respect for the Olympics and what they supposedly stood for.

By the mid-1980s, my little sister, Debbie, had become a pretty good swimmer. In 1986, she was preparing to head to Madrid for the World Aquatics Championships. She came home from practice one day and called me.

"Shirley," she said, "the funniest thing happened at practice today."

"What?" I asked her.

"Well, in preparation for our trip to Spain, they gave us what they called a media training session. They told us that, since we're going to be interviewed over there, we needed to understand exactly how we should behave with the press."

"Really?" I said. I'd never heard of this before. Nobody had ever given me a media training session when I was swimming professionally.

"Yeah," she said. "So they showed us this video, kind of like what to do and what not to do. The first interview they showed us was an example of how to politely and consistently answer questions when a reporter talks to us. In the next example, they showed a clip of you snapping back at a reporter in 1976. And they said, 'This is how *not* to handle things.'"

I just laughed. At that point, it didn't really even matter to me. Ten years after the fact, my own country was using me as an example of how not to behave. Too bad the media training left out the part about what to do when your opponents are clearly cheating.

In 1985, I had met a Huntington Beach lifeguard named Mike. Even though we never had much of a relationship, I unexpectedly became pregnant that year. It was clear that the child would not have a father figure, but I decided to have the baby and start life as a single parent.

About four months into my pregnancy, I got a call from my old friend Sammie Lee, the legendary diver who had had been the first Asian American to win an Olympic gold medal for the United States (at the 1948 Summer Games in London). He was also the first man ever to win back-to-back gold medals in Olympic platform diving. Sammie lived nearby in Huntington Beach, and we had become pals.

"Shirley," he said to me over the phone, "I think I might have a good opportunity for you. The Korean women's swimming team is looking for a coach. They're getting ready for the next Olympics in '88, and I think you'd be good for the job. Because of work visas, you would be allowed to live in Korea for ninety days. I think you should do it. I really think they could benefit from your expertise."

It sounded fun to me. I enjoyed coaching, the money was good, and I did love to travel. I had never been to Korea.

Once I arrived, I was taken to my living quarters—a tiny apartment tucked inside a massive sports complex in a city named Pyongyang, which means "flat land" in Korean. About an hour-long bus ride from Seoul, this was where all of the potential Korean Olympians were training. I met the team the next day, and we got right to work. As I started to run the practices, I realized that I was basically channeling everything Mark had done with me over the years in Mission Viejo. I could still hear him in my head as I ran similar drills and spoke the same encouraging words to swimmers who looked like they held special promise.

Sammie had warned me that, culturally, Korea was very different from what I was used to. For starters, there was a huge language barrier. I'm not sure that the other coaches on the team ever really accepted me, outsider that I was. It didn't seem to matter that I had won a bunch of Olympic medals over the years. I was just this American woman who had come in, and there seemed to be a lack of trust. I didn't let that bother me, though; they were paying me well, and I planned on giving them more than their money's worth.

So I endured the steely gray skies and bleak, cold weather. I stayed the course and tried to work the women's team into something competitive. Every day, I got up early to go to the pool and communicated to the team through interpreters. Occasionally I took the bus into Seoul to do some shopping.

One day at practice, I walked past the men's team and heard the coach severely scolding one of the young male swimmers, really getting in his face. I couldn't imagine what the kid had done to deserve such a tongue-lashing, but it was about to get worse. The coach took out a cigarette lighter and barked an order at the poor kid. I presumed he had told the swimmer to extend his hand, because that's what the young man did. The coach grabbed the swimmer's hand and, holding it palm down, held the lighter's flame to it, burning him. The young man screamed in agony as the rest of his team watched. After several seconds of this torture, the coach snapped the lighter shut and ordered the swimmer back into the water. I was horrified.

When my eighty-ninth day arrived, I was ready to pack up and go home. I was seven months pregnant by then, so I had some preparing to do.

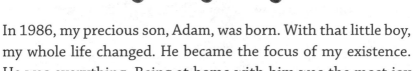

In 1986, my precious son, Adam, was born. With that little boy, my whole life changed. He became the focus of my existence. He was everything. Being at home with him was the most joy I had ever felt in my life. With his red hair and beautiful smile, this child did more for me than any gold medal ever could have. All of the sudden, my life had purpose again. In the little house I'd purchased in Westminster, I learned how to be a mom. I decided then that there would be no more stupid boyfriends or failed relationships.

As a single parent, I learned more about life than I ever could have as a swimmer. Every single moment of every day was built around tending to my little boy. He was all that mattered to me. My past life became a distant memory. The Nationals, the Trials, the endless meets around the world, the Olympics—it all faded away as I focused on my little angel.

In December of 1986, I received the tragic news that my former Olympic teammate, Kim Peyton, one-quarter of our 1976 gold-winning relay team, had died of a brain tumor at just twenty-nine years old. I hadn't kept in touch with her, Wendy, or Jill since the '76 Games, so my last memory of Kim was that of a funny, spirited, tenacious competitor and friend. It was heartbreaking news.

In June of 1987, I was busy at home and trying to make ends meet by working part-time at a sporting goods store when I learned that I was being inducted into the Olympic Hall of Fame. I was even prouder when I found out that, at the same time, Donna de Varona was also being inducted. I had not seen Donna since she interviewed me in 1976 after the famous relay. I had always been such a fan of hers and was still kind of in awe around her.

When Donna and I met up before the ceremony, she pulled me aside and said, "Shirley, I'm sorry."

"Sorry for what?" I asked.

She looked me in the eye and said, "Back in Montreal, everyone should have done more to help you. But we just didn't know what was going on. You deserved better than that."

"No problem, Donna," I told her. "I respect you and what

you've done for the sport and for women. You're still one of my role models, and you don't owe me any apology."

Covering the Olympics for a major broadcast network in the mid-1970s, like Donna did, was not an investigative job. To me, it was up to the newspaper reporters to have covered—and uncovered—the story.

When the 1988 Summer Olympics in Seoul, Korea, came around, I paid attention as usual, wondering just how far the East German swimming program had advanced. By then, it was just expected that they would do well. They had continued to establish themselves as one of the most efficient and success-ful swimming programs in the world, despite the fact that the women looked and sounded like men. The incredible Janet Ev-ans swam wonderfully in Seoul for the United States, winning three individual golds. She had started out training with my old coach, Mark, which made me happy.

But then you had Kristin Otto from East Germany, who be-came the first woman to win *six* gold medals at a single Olympic Games. That had been my own goal in '76. In addition to Ot-to's head-turning performance, the East German women also took gold in the 200-meter breaststroke, 200-meter butterfly, 200-meter individual medley, 4×100-meter freestyle relay, and 4×100-meter medley relay.

Overall, the East German swimmers trounced everybody, including the United States. Our own Matt Biondi had a remark-able run in Korea, winning five golds. But it was not enough to overtake the East Germans, who ended up with a total of twen-ty-eight swimming medals, including eleven gold. The United States wrapped up with eighteen total medals, including eight gold. The East German women helped their country overall in terms of medal count, coming in second behind the Soviet Union. The United States placed third, which stunned me. The East German swimmers were strong as ever.

At the '88 Games, a dozen or so athletes tested positive for banned substances, as usual. But one of them made major news. Sprinter Ben Johnson, who was born in Jamaica and immigrated to Canada in 1976, became a track and field star there and went on to international success in just a few years. At the '84 Games in Los Angeles, he won the bronze in the 100, behind Carl Lewis and Sam Graddy. He also won a bronze in the 4×100 relay.

In the four years that followed, Johnson became a much stronger runner. In 1977, competing at the World Championships in Rome, he gained instant and international fame by beating Carl Lewis for the title while also setting a world record. After that, he got tons of endorsements and was named the Associated Press Athlete of the Year for 1987. But while in Rome, Carl Lewis started explaining to people why he thought he had lost. First, he claimed that Johnson had false-started. Then he said he'd had a bad stomach. But then he dropped a minor bombshell that I could relate to. Without naming any names, Carl Lewis said, "There are a lot of people coming out of nowhere. I don't think they are doing it without drugs."

I appreciated and respected what Lewis had said, even though others criticized him for being a poor sport. I don't know him personally, so I can't speak for his motivation, but I do know that he was a champion and a hard worker. Whenever he spoke up, it was about something important.

Now, it should be noted that in 2003, Lewis did acknowledge that he failed three drug tests during the '88 Olympic Trials, which under international rules should have prevented him from going to the Olympic Games two months later. But it was covered up. According to him, hundreds of American athletes were allowed to escape bans with similar cover-ups. It was just a mess.

After Lewis spoke out about him at the '77 World

Championships, Ben Johnson said, "When Carl Lewis was winning everything, I never said a word against him. And when the next guy comes along and beats me, I won't complain about that, either."

Of course, Johnson's response sparked a rivalry heading straight into the '88 Games. But it was no contest. Johnson took the gold medal, setting a world record with a time of 9.79. The Canadians went crazy. The prime minister, Brian Mulroney, watched the race and called Johnson right away to congratulate him. The Canadian press went wild.

But within forty-eight hours, it was all over. Johnson had tested positive for steroids and was disqualified. Olympic officials confiscated his gold medal, immediately erased the world record, and suspended Johnson from all competitions for two years. Eventually, he would also be stripped of his 1987 world record.

It was a huge story. The situation had obviously gone beyond state-sponsored programs. Now individual athletes were starting to take it upon themselves to cheat.

CHAPTER EIGHTEEN

New Beginnings

By the spring of 1988, I had worked enough odd jobs to know that it was time to start thinking seriously about some sort of career. The only problem was that I had no clue what I should be doing. But I did know that working in a sporting goods store wasn't going to provide much of a future for me and Adam.

One day, my mother came to visit me at my house. Looking out the window at the mailman as he walked up to the door and dropped some envelopes through the slot, she turned to me and said, "What if you just do that?"

It didn't seem like such a crazy idea. Mail people are outside most of the time, and they get great exercise by walking a lot and carrying heavy bags of mail. The job must keep you in shape. What the heck, I thought to myself. I'll give it a shot.

I went down to the Huntington Beach Post Office and took a test along with about five hundred other people. I got more than seventy-five percent of the questions right, which meant that I qualified. A few months went by until they had anything available. One day, I finally got the call and went in for training.

As I would soon learn, letter carriers do a lot more than just carry letters. But I liked the job a lot from the very start. I made some good friends almost right away, and the job itself was interesting to me. It required a lot of concentration, sorting things and figuring out where people lived. But it was also a way for me to spend a lot of time by myself, which I liked, while still making friends back at the post office. I started getting to know people along my route. I learned things about my city I had never known before. For me, it was the best of all worlds.

There were still some people on my route who would recognize my name and ask if I was *that* Shirley Babashoff. My fellow postal workers were always surprised to hear about my history, but thankfully, they didn't make a big deal out of it. I liked where I was. All of the sudden, I had a career where I could remain fairly anonymous but not completely forgotten. That worked for me.

In August of 1961, the communist government of the German Democratic Republic of East Germany had built a barbed wire and concrete wall between East and West Berlin. The stated purpose of the Berlin Wall was to keep out western fascists and prevent mass defections from east to west.

The foreboding and ominous wall, which I had seen up close and personal on my first trip to Europe back in 1971, stood until November 9, 1989. That's when the head of the East German Communist Party announced to the people of the GDR that they were free to cross the border whenever they pleased. That evening, thousands gleefully swarmed the wall. Some crossed easily into West Berlin, while others began destroying the wall with hammers. With that, the most powerful symbol of the Cold War was destroyed.

I watched the event unfold on the news, but I never really thought about its connection to what had happened to me and other athletes in 1976. It would soon become very clear, though.

That same year, my mom died at the age of fifty-six. She had been taking so many pills for so long that I wasn't really surprised when it happened. In a way, I feel bad that she had to live the life that she did. Even though she covered up my father's crimes, in the end, I chalked it up to their generation; it was just what you did for your husband. What a shame that there was nothing in that old-world tradition about protecting your own kids from abuse.

By that time, I had become pretty estranged from my family. After my mom died, we really drifted. My siblings and I barely spoke, and my father had moved down to Dana Point, about forty-five minutes south. I was just focusing on my little boy.

In 1989, the *Los Angeles Times* reported:

> *EAST BERLIN—East Germany, thrusting its new policy of openness into the sports arena, admitted today for the first time that some of its athletes had been exposed in dope tests as drug-takers.*
>
> *Reporting on an unprecedented visit to East Germany's Kreischa doping laboratory near Dresden, newspapers said fourteen positive results were returned by unnamed East German athletes last year in testing at domestic events or in spot checks during training.*

Wow. It was starting to happen. The curtain was being pulled back.

Through reports, we began to learn that in 1965, East Germany had isolated itself from the sporting world in order to hide their government-sponsored program of doping athletes with performance-enhancing drugs. The program was known as State Plan 14.25. The systematic doping, created under the auspices of East Germany's elite Sports Federation and monitored by the Ministry of State Security known as the Stasi, was designed as a master plan to achieve worldwide prestige through sports.

Girls as young as twelve years old had been recruited from all across the country and, without their knowledge, been given male hormones and other untested steroids as part of their training regimen. While the government was intent on winning competitions all over the world, the primary goal was to own the Olympics stage.

By the late 1960s and early '70s, the East German doping program had become highly organized and super efficient while remaining invisible to the rest of the world. German chemists and pharmacists worked tirelessly at a secret lab in Leipzig, developing new forms of anabolic steroids, an artificial testosterone. By then, there were more than three thousand Stasi spies within the system to keep an eye on coaches, scientists, and even athletes to ensure that there were no leaks.

By all accounts, not even the athletes' parents had been aware of what was happening to their children. They were required, in essence, to turn over their offspring to the government without question, for development within the secret muscle-enhancing program.

As the details continued to pour forth, it became worse and worse. In 1991, the *New York Times* reported a story that began:

OLYMPICS; COACHES CONCEDE THAT STEROIDS
FUELED EAST GERMANY'S SUCCESS IN SWIMMING

The stunning domination of international swimming by East German women for nearly two decades was built upon an organized system of anabolic-steroid use, a group of twenty former East German coaches confirmed yesterday.

Their admission, provided to reporters in Bonn, is the

*latest evidence—and some of the most convincing—that se-
nior sports administrators of the now-dissolved Communist
state made performance-enhancing drugs a critical part of
the training programs for the country's elite athletes.*

The article also named some of the athletes who had been
doping, including Kornelia Ender, Petra Schneider, Ute Geweniger, Barbara Krause, and Ulrike Richter, among others. The
names didn't surprise me, though. What caught my eye was
the part that said the athletes wouldn't be losing their medals
or records. Why couldn't the International Olympic Committee
punish them?

One day, soon after the revelations about East Germany, a
camera crew from *20/20* showed up at the post office where I
worked. They wanted to interview me. At first, I refused.

"Shirley," the reporter said to me, "this is such a big moment for you. You knew this all along."

I understood what he was saying, but I also didn't want to
go back in time. I just wasn't ready to be placed at the forefront
of this story and be featured in a bunch of articles and on talk
shows. I didn't want to go back to being that person who was
asked a million questions about the East Germans—that person who, in 1976, had ended up defining who I was in the public eye for the rest of my life.

The bigger the story got, the more my phone rang and rang
with interview requests. Even though I didn't give any interviews, I recall getting a mention in the *Los Angeles Times*—a
little article that simply ended with "Shirley was right." I was
amused by the brief statement; when I had accused the East
Germans of cheating back in 1976, huge headlines had been
splashed all over the world about it. Now that my accusation
was backed by evidence, all I warranted was three words.

One day in early 1992, my supervisor called me into his office. "Shirley," he said, "the United States Postal Service has signed on to be the official carrier of this year's Olympics in Barcelona, and we want to talk to you about it. We think this is a great opportunity for you to help us out."

I had no idea what he was talking about, but I was interested in hearing more. He dialed a number on his phone and told me that we were about to speak to the Postmaster General. What? The U.S. Postmaster General, Marvin Runyon, would be talking to me? I almost couldn't believe it.

Moments later, Mr. Runyon got on the line and began speaking with my postmaster on speakerphone. Soon I was brought into the conversation.

"What do you think about this, Shirley?" Mr. Runyon asked me. "We'd really love your help in getting the word out. Your place in history means a lot to us, and we're proud to have you on our team."

I sat there for a moment in silence, with a lot of thoughts going through my mind. Maybe this was an opportunity to get back in the game, to embrace the Olympics in a way I hadn't been able to for a number of years.

"I think this is a terrific idea," I said to Mr. Runyon. "I would be proud to represent the Postal Service and my country by taking part in something like this. I'll do whatever you'd like me to do, and I'll consider it an honor."

And so it began. The Postal Service worked out a schedule for me to travel around the country for a number of months as an ambassador for the program, making appearances and giving brief speeches. Adam was in kindergarten at the time, and I met with his teacher to ask if he could come with me. She thought it was a great idea.

"He'll learn a lot more with you than he will sitting in a class," she said. "It sounds like a wonderful opportunity."

It was so much fun to travel again, and having Adam with me made it even better. In California, we followed the Olympic torch run in a car, heading north toward Petaluma. Along the way, we stopped at the post offices in various towns and cities to greet the torch. At each stop, I said a few words about how proud I was to be both a former Olympian and a postal carrier.

After our California road trip, Adam and I traveled to Colorado, Florida, Kentucky, South Carolina, Rhode Island, North Dakota, and other states to help spread the word about the Olympics. I was having a great time, and thankfully, nobody brought up the East Germans or any of the negative aspects from the '76 Games. People were still excited to talk about my famous relay race. Many fans recounted it for me the same way they would talk about the 1980 Miracle on Ice hockey game. It had never really struck me just what that race meant to people. I knew what it had meant to me and my teammates, but the fact that others were also moved by it was a very profound thing for me. It was one of the best things I took away from the tour.

That year, I was featured once again in *Sports Illustrated*. The story began with this:

BABASHOFF AND ENDER

At the 1976 Summer Games two of the top female swimmers in the world—an American and an East German—met. The American won only one gold medal, while her rival won four golds. But had the East German used steroids?

Well, I could answer that pretty easily: Yes, she had! For the article, *Sports Illustrated* first came and interviewed me at my home in Fountain Valley. Then they went to Germany to interview Kornelia Ender. Then the reporter and I met with Kornelia in Indianapolis, at the World Masters Championships at Indiana University. Kornelia was still swimming at that point, and was competing at the meet.

Even though I had put the past behind me, when I saw Kornelia at the tournament, I was as chilly to her as I had been back in '76. I couldn't help myself. I had my son Adam with me, and one day he would know the whole story. But at just five years old, he was still too young to understand what his mom had been through.

We also met Kornelia's husband, East German decathlete Steffen Grummt. He was a nice guy and played with Adam a lot. Kornelia and I ended up having dinner together, and while it was more pleasant than I expected, it also felt kind of superficial. In the back of my mind, I was wondering if she would own up to what the East Germans had done, or least accept the fact that maybe things hadn't been done fairly sixteen years earlier. But it never came up.

In the *Sports Illustrated* article, the writer quoted my reaction to any uncertainty that Kornelia had taken steroids before the '76 Games: "Firmly she replied, 'I'm certain. There is no doubt in my mind. Sure, I believe in talent, but don't ask me to believe she was the only one who didn't take them.'"

The thing I remember most from the writer's interview with me was that he still couldn't wrap his head around what had happened. He still couldn't ask the hard questions, despite having an athlete right there in front of him who had been doped by her own country. Oh well, I thought to myself. Maybe nobody would ever care again, and that's just the way it was. Maybe there would never be any hard proof that they had cheated. I knew it in my heart, and the news reports seemed to support it. But the East German athletes themselves were having none of it. They were still ignoring the obvious.

In April of 1998, another article appeared in the *New York Times*.

IN A COLD WAR HANGOVER, GERMANY CONFRONTS A LEGACY OF STEROIDS

BERLIN—For decades during the cold war, outsiders watched in frustration, rage, envy, or astonishment as East German athletes accumulated gold medals, powering their way to record-breaking triumphs in sports from swimming to the shot-put. Many suspected drugs were fueling the success. But few of those suspicions could be definitively proved.

Now, in Courtroom 700 of Berlin's state courthouse, more than seven years after Germany's reunification, prosecutors are seeking to expose some of the most closely guarded secrets of that long, murky era.

The article detailed the documents from the former communist secret police, which revealed what I had suspected back in the 1970s: that the state-sponsored campaign to dope its athletes had wanted to win Olympic gold as proof of communism's supremacy.

It was a far more elaborate case than anybody had imagined, even me. Four coaches and two doctors were accused of causing deep harm to at least nineteen East German athletes by forcing them to use steroids. Nineteen female athletes appeared as witnesses and most of them described what the drugs had done to them, including deepening their voices and growing extreme body hair. The secret files also revealed that some of the women had actually been ordered to abort fetuses that may have been harmed by the drugs. And that was just beginning. The *Times* later reported that East Germany had provided performance-enhancing drugs to as many as 10,000 athletes from 1968 to 1988.

In 1998, the United States Olympic Committee sought to have formal Olympic medals given to American athletes who had lost out to East German athletes. An "upgrade" of sorts. This was amazing. But was it possible?

"We think it's a matter of fundamental fairness," said Bill Hybl, president of the United States Olympic Committee.

But Jacques Rogge, an influential member of the International Olympic Committee from Belgium, had other ideas. "There is absolutely not going to be any change for things that happened more than ten years ago," he said. "At this stage, we still have no documented evidence of doping of an athlete on the day of Olympic competitions."

Sadly, Rogge was right. A month later, *Swimming World* reported that the International Olympic Committee had decided not to give medals or recognition to the U.S. swimmers who had lost to the East Germans, even in light of the proof that they had taken performance-enhancing drugs. The United States Olympic Committee, the magazine reported, would find "appropriate medal recognition" for the members of the U.S. medley relay team that had lost to the East Germans at the '76 Games: me, Linda Jezek, Lauri Siering, and Camille Wright.

With that decision, it felt as if the final gate had come down and the discussion was closed. I thought the International Olympic Committee was being terribly irresponsible by completely writing us all off. But I understood why—it was embarrassing and made the Olympics look bad. I think that's why they didn't want to deal with it. They didn't want to go back and open up that can of worms again. But if they had done it, it never would have been mentioned again. It would have actually been a triumphant moment in Olympics history. It would have clearly illustrated that the International Olympic Committee was actually committed to doing what was right, and wasn't afraid to give credit where it was due. Clearly, they didn't consider what it was like to dedicate so much of your life to your chosen sport, and then get cheated out of the recognition you deserved for all your hard work. That dedication seemed lost on them. It reminded me once again why I didn't want to be involved in the Olympics anymore.

Later in 1998, *Swimming World* reported a breaking story:

FORMER EAST GERMAN COACH
ADMITS TO DOPING ATHLETES

BERLIN, GERMANY—In the latest confession of doping from former East German sports figures, the former national women's swim coach admitted in court that he secretly gave his athletes banned performance-enhancing drugs. Rolf Glaeser, fifty-eight, who has worked as a coach in Austria since 1990, also apologized to his former swimmers. Several former East German coaches and doctors have recently admitted to doping during the former communist country's state-sponsored drive to produce Olympic champions. In a case last week, two former East German coaches and a doctor were convicted of giving anabolic steroids to unwitting athletes, some as young as twelve. The charges carry a maximum of three years in prison, but the sports officials convicted last week received only fines after confessing and apologizing.

CHAPTER NINETEEN

The Cheaters

The home run race between Mark McGwire and Sammy
Sosa in 1998 was so celebrated and revered that many credit-
ed it with helping bring fans back to baseball after the strike
of 1995. And who couldn't get caught up in the excitement of
those two guys chasing such a famous record?

The thing was, though, Mark McGwire did not look right
to me. He lived near me in Huntington Beach while the race
was going on, and though I didn't know him, I sort of followed
him in sports because he was a local guy. When I saw those
arms of his on TV, it didn't make sense to me. I remembered
watching him play early in his career, and he had been this tall,
skinny kid. Working out is one thing, but this was something
different and it didn't feel right to me. I got the same little suspicious twinge I'd had back in the mid-1970s, when I noticed
the East German girls. As an athlete, you just have a sense for
these things. You know what it takes to work out and get your
body in that kind of shape.

As it turned out, the home run race was a fraud. Sure, it
was fun to watch, but it wasn't real. McGwire stated in 2005,
under oath, that he'd been taking an anabolic steroid precursor
called androstenedione, a substance that, at the time, had been
banned by the International Olympic Committee and the NFL

but not the MLB.

A few years later, Sosa tested positive for a performance-enhancing drug after claiming that he only took vitamins. Then, during a congressional hearing in 2005, McGwire said that although he'd taken steroids periodically for almost ten years, the drugs had not helped him hit home runs.

This was all the result of José Canseco's 2005 book, *Juiced*, in which Canseco admitted to using anabolic steroids and also claimed that up to eighty-five percent of major league players also juiced. In the book, Canseco specifically accused former teammates Mark McGwire, Rafael Palmeiro, Jason Giambi, Iván Rodríguez, and Juan González as fellow cheaters, even claiming that he had injected them himself. Some of the players denied it, but then soon on Capitol Hill, we began to see things differently as players (including McGwire) fumbled and seemed to make excuses.

Canseco took a lot of flak for his accusations against these athletes. Admittedly, ratting people out is not a great thing to do, but think about how different baseball and other sports might have been if his book hadn't spotlighted the issue.

I know this wasn't state-sponsored doping. But it was still cheating. The older I got, the less I believed that athletes in general could be satisfied with simply working hard and performing well based on their own strengths. I had been naive, I thought, to believe that this was possible. Whenever I read a news article about another athlete getting busted, my mind would jerk back to my twenty-mile swimming days for all those years before the '76 Olympics. Did anybody care about doing things the right way anymore? More importantly, did any of the athletes who have been accused of doping ever give a single thought to their status as role models, and what this might make kids want to do? I understand the will to win. But they completely ignored the influence they had and what the ramifications of their actions might be. We'll probably never know all the damage caused by these selfish athletes.

In July of 2000, the *New York Times* published this in an article:

> *The former head of East German sports was convicted to-day of directing the "systematic and overall doping" of the nation's Olympic athletes in a secret program that ravaged their bodies.*
>
> *A court found that Manfred Ewald, seventy-four, the former East German sports chief, and Manfred Hoeppner, sixty-five, the longtime medical director, shared responsibility for the steroid program that ran from 1974 until the Berlin Wall came down in 1989.*

This was really getting to be something. The East Germans were starting to take it seriously. I started to wonder how close-ly the International Olympic Committee was following this story. Was there any possibility of re-awarding the medals from the '76 Games to the many athletes who had been cheated?

In 2004, I made a surprise appearance at a luncheon before the Olympic Trials in Long Beach. My old coach, Mark, was there too, and it was great to catch up with him. I also gave my first interview in eight years. It felt good to speak out, to put my toe back in the water, so to speak. I wanted justice, not only for myself, but also for all of those other swimmers. I was happy with how the *USA Today* article turned out. It told the story well. Here's an excerpt from it:

> *In the summer of 1976, in one of the sports media's most shameful moments, Babashoff was painted as more of a villain than the East Germans, incredibly enough. Back then, she talked to reporters, dozens of them, and she was brutally honest. She was the first American to speak out about*

steroids, the first to point an accusatory finger at the East Germans.

For her honesty and insight, Babashoff wasn't lauded. She was mercilessly criticized by a press corps that had never dealt with steroid accusations of this magnitude. It was all too new. Babashoff even earned herself a nickname from the media: Surly Shirley.

The media was also starting to understand that it wasn't just us Americans who had been victimized. In 1998, John Powers of the *Boston Globe* had written:

Shirley Babashoff should have been America's golden girl at the 1976 Summer Olympics . . . Now, after a decade of admissions by former GDR coaches, doctors, and swimmers and findings in two recent German criminal trials, the Americans want what they believe they were cheated out of twenty-two years ago.

Despite the calls from our side, the IOC simply didn't seem willing to budge on any level. By then, even the East German athletes had started speaking out. In the book *The Olympic Games: A Social Science Perspective*, famed breaststroke swimmer Renate Vogel shared some horrific details about what her government did to her:

The blue pills started after the 1972 Olympics in Munich. In the 1973 season we began to get injections also. We were given two injections per week when we were in training camp. No one was sure which shots were the steroids because we were also pumped full of vitamin B, C, and D in the beginning and didn't really think anything of it. You know, when you are around other athletes like yourself, you don't notice the difference in body size. There were very few

people on the team who thought about it or really cared.
They were of the opinion that the main thing was to swim
quickly, and it didn't matter how. I started to notice the ef-
fect of the steroids when my clothes didn't fit anymore. This
was the beginning of 1973. In retrospect I can see that I had
really broad shoulders. I went from a size forty to forty-four
or larger. My period hardly ever came.

Renate had competed against us in Belgrade back in 1973, where she had won two gold medals. She eventually set two world records, too. In 1979, she fled to West Germany, where she eventually opened up about what had been done to her and her teammates.

As the truth spread about what had happened at the '76 Games, people began stopping me on the street and asking for my thoughts on the issue. I turned down a lot of interviewers in the late 1990s and early 2000s. I just didn't want to talk about it. I know people thought I was bitter and angry and unable to deal with what had happened. But that really wasn't it. I had simply compartmentalized that part of my life; I had been able to put it away in a place where it couldn't bother me anymore. I had my son, my new life as a mail carrier, and new friends, none of whom had anything to do with swimming. I knew that those interviews would just open up old wounds. Thankfully, my co-workers at the post office never bothered me about it. They didn't care about my past. They accepted me for who I was now, in the present.

On the inside, I was thrilled that the truth was finally coming out. The press was proving that it could now at least view an issue honestly and even investigate it relentlessly if it needed to. The media had come a long way since the '70s.

Unfortunately, doping was still rampant. As big as this story was, it still seemed like I would read about some new performance-enhancement drug scandal in the newspaper every other day. There was a bigger issue that needed to be discussed about the importance of morals and playing by the rules. It seemed like those concepts had become old-fashioned. Society put so much emphasis on winning. That "win at any cost" mentality was, of course, driven by the amount of money that could be made. I don't think anybody would argue that most professional sports have been completely taken over by the pull of money. That's the name of the game. It seemed like people would do whatever it took to succeed in sports, no matter how dangerous it was to their bodies.

The *New York Times* and *Swimming World* in particular continued to provide updates and amazing coverage of what was happening with the doping story. The piece I remember best was written by Karen Crouse, who is now a highly respected sports writer for the *New York Times*. In 2004, Crouse approached me about writing a feature for the *Palm Beach Post*, the newspaper she worked for at the time. She came to California to interview me and spend some time with me, and then produced a piece that many still cite today for its scope, depth, and incredible writing. Here is a small portion of it:

> *Over lunch at the Harbor House Cafe in Sunset Beach, Babashoff picks at her past in the same way she does the heaping bowl of salad greens in front of her. She chews contentedly on some memories and absently pushes bitter ones aside.*
>
> *She's considered swimming's version of Greta Garbo, this despite the fact that she interacts with the public every day in her job as a letter carrier in Huntington Beach.*

Babashoff, forty-seven, has become one of those people who's hiding in plain sight.

It wasn't like that in 1976. Before the Olympics she graced the Sports Illustrated *cover. And after? She was recognized everywhere she went. People would point at her and sneer, "There's Surly Shirley."*

Babashoff was guilty of a false start. She jumped the gun in outing steroid users. The outspoken Californian was years ahead of the IOC hierarchy in confronting the cartoonishly muscular competitors who kept beating her to the finish. She was decades ahead of the U.S. Anti-Doping Agency in indicting athletes without positive proof, on the strength of "non-analytical positives," if you will.

CHAPTER TWENTY

The Olympic Order

I received the Olympic Order on April 30, 2005, an honor that the International Olympic Committee calls "the highest award of the Olympic Movement."

That day, IOC members Bob Ctvrtlik, Anita DeFrantz, and Jim Easton presented the award to me. I was quite honored. The IOC had established the Olympic Order in 1974 to honor individuals who have illustrated the Olympic ideals through their actions, have achieved remarkable merit in the sporting world, or have rendered outstanding services to the Olympic cause, either through their own personal achievements or their contributions to the development of sport. But had I really done all that, or was this some kind of payback for what had happened in 1976?

In the back of my mind, I felt like they were using the Olympic Order as a way to shut me up or at least placate me and make me think everything was okay. I had made a few comments around that time, and I'm sure they knew that I was considering speaking more of my mind. Don't get me wrong, I was truly honored and I know how special that award is. But I would much rather have the IOC take a good hard look at changing the records.

Soon after I received the Olympic Order, 190 East German

athletes launched a case against the German pharmaceutical giant Jenapharm, claiming that the East German firm knowingly supplied the steroids that were given to them by trainers and coaches from the 1960s through East Germany's demise in 1989. Jenapharm argued that it was not responsible for the doping scandal and blamed the communist system. I was happy to read about this. Finally, the very athletes who had been poisoned were now fighting back.

And it was *Swimming World* that had really embraced the cause once the athletes won their lawsuit. I just owe them so much for the support and attention. This excerpt is from an article they published in early 2007:

> *Now, thirty-one years later, Germany has ended the speculation and proved that the outspoken Babashoff and her teammates were right all along.*
>
> *The payment to 167 of the 10,000 athletes ends a long dispute in Germany. What is interesting is that the unified Germany could have washed its hands of the entire issue by claiming that it was from a previous government no longer in existence.*
>
> *In her own words, Babashoff lays out the case that the issue really isn't over: "Everyone should be compensated somewhat or just acknowledged. Even our own Olympic Committee should step up and have an event where they can invite those who are still alive and recognize them, perhaps with a commemorative medal . . . or at least say, 'We know that this has been hard for you.' They should at least acknowledge the women.*
>
> *"Some people want to think that the issue is over. From our side of it, the whole issue has been shoved under the carpet. I think it is sad. So many women deserved their medals. They were cheated out of their medals at the Olympics!*

"We would like to get what we earned. We were going for the medals, NOT the cash. We were amateurs. We worked so hard. We earned it and it was stolen right in front of everyone's face and no one did anything about it. It was like watching a bank robbery where they just let the crooks go and then say, 'It's okay.'"

In November 2007, I was invited to present the award of Female Athlete of the Year at the fourth annual Golden Goggle Awards held at the Beverly Hills Hotel in Los Angeles. Co-presenting the award with me was my old van-riding partner from the 1976 Olympics, Bruce Jenner.

It was always strange for me to go back into the swimming world for award shows or other events that I was invited to. I always felt like a stranger at those things. But still, I would go occasionally, if for no other reason than to have a nice night out and the chance to see a familiar face or two from a life I once led.

Seeing Bruce Jenner again was kind of a trip. At that point, he had become the king of reality TV along with the rest of his family and extended family, the Kardashians. When we met backstage before heading out to the podium to give the award, I laughed and said, "Why, Bruce, I see you on TV all the time." He looked at me without smiling, shrugged his shoulders, and said, "Hey, a guy's got to make a living."

Not long before the 2008 Olympics, someone told me that our 1976 relay race for the gold medal had been posted on YouTube. I turned on my computer, found the video, and was then transported back in time. I'd never seen the footage of our race before. Of course, I had my perspective of it—my own angle and view of how everything had looked. It was an amazing experience to see what the rest of the world had seen, to hear the words of Donna de Varona and Curt Gowdy, to watch us all getting ready on the pool deck. I could barely wrap my head around it. To see Kim, alive and swimming, was thrilling and bittersweet. Watching the race unfold, hearing the crowd, and watching us power through to the gold was an absolute thrill. I watched it again and again, and all the memories of that magical night flooded back. And the comments beneath the video were very supportive. People seemed to understand, and that made me feel really good.

In 2013, *Swimming World* published something that really caught my eye: an interview with my former coach at the '76 Games, Jack Nelson. As I've already said, I didn't have great respect for this man or how he had coached our team. It was nothing personal, just a fundamental disagreement with his style, strategy, and pretty much everything else he had shared with us. When I read the *Swimming World* article, it confirmed what I had always thought: that our coaches totally let us down at the '76 Olympics. The article began with this:

> BRENT RUTEMILLER: Swimming World Magazine *first reported in 1973—now this is three years out from '76 as you know—that something was going on and everybody was trying to find out what was so special about the East German training program. And in the article there was the first print mentioned that they were experimenting with some type of recovery or fatigue vaccine where they were injecting toxins and there also were some allegations of doping. And at the time that was the first time that it was really brought out that something kind of unusual was going on. Do you remember that period in '73, which is some three years out now?*
>
> JACK NELSON: *Keep in mind that that might have been the*

first time that it was published but we knew but we just couldn't prove it. We knew while we were there that they were beating up on us with steroids and whatever and there was nothing we could do about it, right? Plus we didn't want to be the nasty Americans at the Olympics.

It was infuriating. Like a lot of people, Jack Nelson had been fully aware of what was going on with the East Germans back then. So why hadn't he said something? Nobody—not Coach Nelson nor anyone else—had stood up for me when I spoke out.

JN: *I might be jumping here a little bit but we rode on the same bus from the dormitories as the East Germans and the East Germans were deep voice talking like this and they had hair all over their arms deep voice and like when we get into the Olympic pool Hattie comes flying out and says, "Coach, there are men in the locker room," and I said, "Honey, those aren't men, those are women." And so they had a lot to overcome, psychologically they had a lot to overcome.*

BR: *Let's talk about the media a little bit, because Shirley spoke out and you already said that there was this air where you felt that you were kind of pinned in, you were muzzled, you couldn't really say anything that was derogatory because you would have been branded poor sports, but Shirley said something and as a result she was branded by the media.*

JN: *I mean that woman, that girl, that beautiful athlete was doing some fantastic swimming and no one would appreciate it, no one would get on and say, "Hey lady, you are great," you know what I'm saying?*

Later on in the interview, the reporter asked Nelson what

should be done to compensate us for the 1976 Games. Here's what he said:

> JN: *What a tough question, right? What a tough question, because no way will we ever give them what they totally deserve, but the Olympic Committee surely should give them gold medals for the events where they broke world records. You with me?*
>
> *And the United States Women should give gold medals to the hundreds and the other events that broke American records. Now this in itself is not going to be the most wonderful thing that can happen for our girls, but at least it will remind them that we care about them, that we appreciate them, that they were greater than the people that supposedly touched them out.*
>
> *They were absolutely greater than the people who supposedly touched them out, and in some way or another, that has to be handled properly and realistically because it's unfair, it's unfair and it hurts so much that our great American girls had worked so beautifully to overcome what they were about to have to compete with and nobody—I shouldn't say nobody—but very, very, very few people were willing to step forth and say, "Good job, guys." It's something that should never ever be put aside.*

My biggest issue with Jack Nelson, beyond his lack of support when I spoke out against the East Germans, was what he might have cost me at the Olympics. If Coach Mark had been with me for those three weeks of training camp at West Point, I would have performed even better at the Olympics. I'm all but sure of it. The least Nelson could have done was respect the directions that Mark had given him for my training. But he ignored everything. The athlete/coach relationship can be a sacred one, and it was for Mark and me. I wish Nelson had respected that.

I was as disappointed as everyone else when I learned how Lance Armstrong had allegedly been making his living. It seemed like he was constantly being challenged by people about his performances and facing allegations of doping, but he staunchly denied them all. After a federal inquiry that took place from 2010 to 2012, the United States Anti-Doping Agency accused him not just of doping, but also of drug trafficking, based on many blood samples and eyewitness testimonies from many people, including former teammates. Yet he still denied everything.

When Lance went on the *Oprah Winfrey Show* in January 2013 and admitted to using performance-enhancing drugs, it wasn't much of a surprise to anyone. He'd been using throughout most of his career, including all seven Tour de France wins. This was really depressing for me. Lance was an athlete sponsored by the United States Postal Service, and the organization had put a lot of money into him. They had invested in his reputation and his amazing story as a cancer survivor who also happened to be the best in his sport.

For years, *Swimming World* had been calling attention to the issue of doping in sports, including the situation at the '76 Games. In 2013, they stepped up their efforts even higher, writing amazing features bursting with facts and figures about what was happening and what they felt needed to be done about it. When the IOC called for Lance Armstrong to return the bronze medal he had won in the 2000 Olympics, *SW* was right on top of what it could mean for the '76 Olympics situation. Their headline read:

ARMSTRONG STRIPPED OF OLYMPIC MEDAL,
SETS PRECEDENT FOR IOC TO REVISIT 1976

In December 2013, after years of urging the IOC to take back the medals won by the East German women's swimming team at the '76 Olympics, *Swimming World* made a groundbreaking move: they went ahead and made their own judgments on what they felt should happen to the medals awarded at the '76 Games:

STRIPPED! SWIMMING WORLD VACATES AWARDS
OF GDR DRUG-FUELED SWIMMERS

Based on a mix of positive tests, personal admissions, as well as doping admissions from their coaches, Swimming World Magazine *has stripped Kornelia Ender, Ulrike Tauber, Petra Schneider, Ute Geweniger, and Kristin Otto of their World Swimmer of the Year awards from the 1970s and '80s. Those five swimmers—along with Barbara Krause, Cornelia Sirch, Silke Horner, and Anke Mohring—have had their European Swimmer of the Year awards vacated as well.*

The article went on to describe the magazine's own coverage of the "East German doping machine," starting with an article they published back in 1994 that had reported irrefutable evidence that the members of the East German women's swimming team were the victims of systematized doping. It also listed the athletes who had been cheated out of medals because of doping. The article ended with this:

During the next five days, Swimming World *will remind the world of the pain caused—and continually endured— by those most affected by these drug cheats' continued presence in the record books. The German government has*

*already made the most damning admission with its settle-
ment with 197 former East German athletes to share $2.2
million to address any health issues they might have suffered due to the rampant doping.*

I almost couldn't believe what I was reading. But there it
was. Someone in the media had finally had the guts to do what
was right. No matter what happens after this article comes
out, I thought to myself, the world will finally have an in-depth
piece of journalism written in support of every athlete who was
cheated at those Games.

CHAPTER TWENTY-ONE

The Truth Comes Out

More and more people were going on record about the East German doping program and why it was so devastating. Books were published and documentaries made about it. I often found myself in the center of many of these pieces, sort of like the point person that everything revolves around. I understood why they focused on me, but I felt like the focus should have been on the East German athletes. I felt sick when I thought about them growing older and having families, and then having to endure the physical horrors that are the result of doping. The illnesses and mutations that were clearly connected to those early years of doping were now paying horrific dividends.

I have to admit that, to this day, it still bothers me that none of the East German female swimmers have outwardly admitted to the degree of cheating that went on. I do realize that they may have endured some sort of brainwashing in their early and formative years that could have made it almost impossible for them to separate fiction from reality. I'm not sure I would have been any different, under the same circumstances.

I tried to put myself in their shoes—being told, at ten years old, to take a little blue pill because it would help you swim. The people in charge explaining to you why it's so important to be a better swimmer. Having it drilled into your brain that the stronger you are, the more powerful you will make your country. Suffering through the pressures and techniques that would have controlled a young mind.

In 2014, former East German sprinter Ines Geipel shared some of her own personal hell in an interview with *Deutsche Welle* magazine. It seemed that the East Germans had been doping more than just their swimmers:

> INES GEIPEL: *East Germany was a small, closed-off country with a dictatorship and by the start of the 1970s it was recognized internationally. In 1974, the government derived a national plan where they decided that all athletes in elite sports squads would be given male sexual hormones. That means kids from eight years of age, right up into the national teams. That was around 15,000 people, none of whom had an alternative. You couldn't say, "I'm not going to do it."*

In a way, I did understand what it had been like for the East Germans. They had been victims in the hands of their government; I had been a victim in my home. It was a similar form of cruelty and control.

With that said, when you are the one out there getting cheated over and over, and those competing against you still show no remorse or contrition even after all the evidence comes out against them, it's hard to forgive completely. There has to be a point when, as an adult, you realize what happened to you, and the ramifications of it. Every single swimmer at those Olympics was affected by the cheating of East Germany. I wish that at least a few of the more high-profile swimmers would own up to what happened or, if nothing else, say that they understand what the other swimmers went through.

In January 2014, to mark the twenty-fifth anniversary of

the fall of the Berlin Wall, *Swimming World* and SwimVortex .com wrote a joint letter asking FINA to "recognize all victims during the DDR Olympic reign."

Dear FINA Board Members:

In December, Swimming World Magazine *made the decision to strip its World and European Swimmer of the Year titles awarded to any East German (DDR) female swimmer dating back to 1973. The magazine is revisiting how it might reallocate those awards.*

The decision to strip those titles generated many comments and discussions within the swimming community worldwide. Almost everyone agreed that the systematic doping of athletes by the East German government affected the Olympics medal standings.

Swimming World acknowledged that the DDR women were just as much victims as were the swimmers who were cheated out of winning medals and their place in history. In an article running parallel to Swimming World's *campaign, SwimVortex.com noted the difference between perpetrators of crime and victims of a crime who won medals as a result of the system they were a part of. The fact that there were victims on both sides of the podium goes to the core of the IOC's dilemma in rectifying history.*

On behalf of the swimming community worldwide, we are calling on FINA to recognize all victims during this dark period in Olympic history and to lobby the International Olympic Committee to take similar action.

When Nelson Mandela passed away of late, his story reminded us all of the need to acknowledge the past and then leave it in the past so that reconciliation and healing can take place and a new beginning made. Without acknowledgement, swimming cannot move on.

We therefore ask the following:

1. *That FINA acknowledge that the aquatic records were tainted during the DDR era.*
2. *That FINA acknowledge that there were victims on both sides of the podium.*
3. *That FINA place an asterisk next to all DDR era swimmers, explaining that they were unknowingly doped.*
4. *That FINA acknowledge a second tier of new medal standings (consisting of those not recognized) alongside the existing standings of DDR victims.*
5. *That FINA not ask for DDR swimmers to return their medals.*
6. *That FINA award duplicate medals to those athletes who have a new standing.*
7. *That FINA remove from its list of Pin winners all GDR officials, including the convicted Dr. Lothar Kipke, a former Medical Commission delegate who was found guilty of harm to minors in the German doping trials of the late 1990s.*
8. *That FINA stage an event where those who are affected by the reordering of the medals meet with the DDR women in a spirit of sportsmanship, consolation, and forgiveness.*

The final request above could be the most impactful for all parties and victims. We cannot think of anything more powerful, emotional, and meaningful than FINA staging a medal ceremony during the 2015 World Championships. A ceremony of this nature speaks to all that is good about forgiveness, sportsmanship, and above all the spirit of humanity.

Respectfully Signed,

Craig Lord
Publisher: SwimVortex

Brent T. Rutemiller
Publisher: Swimming World Magazine

The letter made excellent points. But, predictably, nothing was done in response to this powerful call for action.

In the summer of 2014, I was contacted by my old friend Mike Unger from Team USA Swimming. He told me about a documentary that was in the works called *The Last Gold*, which would tell the story of the women's 4x100 freestyle relay at the '76 Games. It was being directed by fifteen-time Emmy winner Brian Brown, a talented man who had helped shape NBC's broadcasts of the Olympic Games.

I sat down with Brian and did a couple of interviews for the documentary. He asked me thoughtful questions that really got to the heart of what had happened back then. I could tell that he was a man with a vision and was doing something really great for the sport.

Eventually, Brian's production team came to my house to help me go through my old boxes of swimming stuff, looking for photos and film clips they could use for the film. It was during one of those afternoons that we discovered a whole bunch of Super 8 home movie reels that had been shot by my family and friends over the years. It was amazing to see all of those old clips of me as a teenager. The material was shipped back East and soon returned to me as a DVD.

I was really happy that there was such a talented team

working on the production. They interviewed everybody involved in the '76 Games, from my teammates to some of the
East German athletes who had been doping back then. There
had been so many times when I thought the world had forgotten, and that our story would never be told. Then, all of the sudden, a group like this steps up and creates something so special
and honest and raw and real that you almost can't believe it.

When I think back to the '76 Olympics, I wonder how the
event will be remembered, or whether future generations will
learn that steroids—at least, what we think of as steroids today—really sort of began at those Games.

In November 2014, I read in the paper that Jack Nelson had
died. The *New York Times* obituary on him included this:

> *Nelson's strategy to upend the East German winning streak*
> *was one of matchups and goals. He sent the best American*
> *sprinter, Kim Peyton, out first, to stay within a body length*
> *of the East German star Kornelia Ender. The task of the*
> *second swimmer, Wendy Boglioli, was to make up the body*
> *length. It was the third swimmer, Jill Sterkel, who was as-*
> *signed to grab the lead, and the anchor, Shirley Babashoff,*
> *a distance specialist who had been especially frustrated by*
> *the East Germans' dominance, who was charged with keep-*
> *ing it.*

So there he was, still getting so much credit for our winning
the relay. That just was not my experience. But there something else in the obituary that was far more serious than taking
credit for a relay race.

But late in his career, his reputation was tainted when he was accused by one of his most prominent former swimmers, Diana Nyad, of having repeatedly molested her when she was a teenager.

I had heard rumors about this over the years and for obvious reasons, it was particularly upsetting to me. I had grown up with a sexual predator and was aware of the fact that many of them were coaches preying on young athletes, in probably every sport there is. Nelson had been a father figure to many swimmers over the years at his training facilities in Florida, and I know that many of my teammates had enjoyed working with him during the 1976 Olympics. Nelson denied the charges made against him.

The *New Times Broward-Palm Beach* reported this story:

In 1989, Nyad appeared on the live TV talk show People Are Talking *with the caption "Raped by Coach" beneath her name. Intensely angry still, she recounted Nelson's abuse, saying it began when she was fourteen. He told her that she started it by writing "I love Coach Nelson" on her notebook, she said, and that their relationship was so special that no one else would understand.*

For years afterwards, Nyad would recount, in sickeningly vivid detail, what she claimed Coach Nelson had done to her. She was quoted in the aforementioned article:

"[Nelson] started saying, 'It doesn't matter what you swim . . . We're not going to talk about that . . . Look at these beautiful breasts of yours." Nelson took her into a small bathroom attached to his office, Nyad says, and again tried to penetrate her. "'I need this. I'm a grown man,'" Nyad says she was told.

I can't see any reason why Diana would have made all of this up. To me, all of Coach Nelson's denials fell flat. It was tragically ironic to me that the coach whom I felt had really let me down during the Olympics may also have been a sexual predator. It was depressing to me. I suddenly felt especially blessed that I had been coached by Flip Darr and Mark Schubert.

In 2009, my father had once again been arrested as a sex offender. He had been at the harbor in Dana Point, looking at children through binoculars from his truck. At eighty-one years old, he was still stalking children.

In the summer of 2015, I was informed that someone had filed a restraining order against my father. I asked a friend of mine to go to the hearing that morning for me. Afterward, he described to me what had happened. What made my father's actions even more heinous was the fact that the person in question was a mentally challenged woman in her early forties. She had built a life for herself working as a supermarket clerk near my father's house.

After the hearing, at which the judge did in fact impose a restraining order, my friend spoke to the woman's parents, who seemed quite shaken. They explained to him how upsetting it all had been. They had heard about this strange, elderly man who had approached their daughter in the supermarket where she worked and offered to give her money and drive her home. Then they had found him lurking outside of the group home where she lived some thirty minutes away from the market. They had no idea if my father had done anything physical to their daughter yet.

When my friend told me all of this, many of those horrific memories came flooding back. It also made me think back to when my father was released in the mid-1970s. My mom told us that he had received counseling for his predatory behavior. "Dad was in treatment, so he is probably okay now," she said. But I don't think you can cure child predators. I really don't. In my opinion, given my father's history, there was absolutely no reason that he should not have been locked up for the rest of his life. They had caught him this time. But what about the other times when nobody saw him spying? What else had he been up to down there in Dana Point?

The police never once approached me or spoke to me about my father, not even when I was a child. This leads me to believe that the system is woefully broken in this country. In the news, I'll read about some teenager getting locked up for having sex with someone his own age, yet monsters like my father run free. We need to look at these situations carefully and on an individual basis. There are stalkers and predators who do not belong out on the streets, and my father is one of them.

When I first sat down to write this book, I wasn't sure if I would include any of this as part of my story. But in the end, there was no way to ignore it. I hope the story of my own experience will help others who have been through the same kind of torture, both in bedrooms and in locker rooms. It's so easy for people to take advantage of kids. We need to do something about it. Once it happens, these kids cannot be fixed; they're permanently broken.

CHAPTER TWENTY-TWO

My Future Is Now

As time went on, I felt as if life had started being kinder to me. After the media and so many others finally acknowledged that my teammates and I had been cheated at the 1976 Olympics, I was able to reflect on, analyze, and even just appreciate all of the great things I'd had the opportunity to be a part of. I could look back on that time with pride, knowing that my teammates and I had always played by the rules.

In early 2015, I had lunch with my old coach, Mark. I hadn't seen him since the Olympic Trials in Long Beach ten years prior. I don't why, but I was little nervous heading over to the restaurant in Huntington Beach. I'd always had so much respect for Mark.

When I walked into the restaurant and saw him sitting there, it took me back to our days down in Mission Viejo. We reminisced for a couple of hours about those hundreds of practices, and all of the good times we'd had traveling and working together. We also talked about the day I had temporarily decided to quit, a month before the 1976 Olympic Trials.

"You really scared me when you left that day," Mark said. "But in my heart I didn't think you were really going to go through with it. I think you were doing what a lot of teenagers would have done in that moment. You just snapped a little bit.

Honestly, I'm amazed it didn't happen to you earlier. You had so much pressure on you and the weight of the world on your back." He smiled at me. "Aren't you glad you didn't quit?"

"Absolutely," I said.

Like me, Mark felt very strongly about what the IOC still needed to do.

"Shirley," he said, "don't be afraid to keep making waves about this. I know they haven't listened to lots of others in the past, but you were the one that it affected the most. You were really the scapegoat. Maybe they will listen to you."

In 2014, *Newsweek* published a remarkably comprehensive piece on the East German doping scandal, revealing even more about the country's well-organized training system for its athletes and the little blue pill at the core of it. The damage those little blue pills did just went on for decades. Is the International Olympic Committee paying attention? I wondered. What other proof did they need that something had to be done about the 1976 Games?

Maybe it will never end. Maybe my teammates and I will never have the satisfaction of a full resolution.

Just as I was finishing up this book, I received a call from my friend, sports journalist Karen Crouse. She was working on a story for the *New York Times* and wanted to see if I would give her a couple of quotes for it. I asked her what her article was about, and she told me that the World Anti-Doping Agency had just released a massive 323-page report laying out details about an extensive state-sponsored doping program in Russia involving track and field athletes. The report recommended that Russia be suspended from the 2016 Olympics if it did not impose extreme improvements to its anti-doping efforts. It also recommended barring five athletes and five officials from the Olympics for life.

There we were, in 2015, facing another state-sponsored

doping program. Wow. Here was more of the same mysterious and dishonest manipulation. I thought about all of the clean Russian athletes and what it must have been like for them the day the report was released.

I read the details of the case after talking to Karen, and it was even worse than I'd thought. There were reports that tests from athletes were routinely prescreened at a shady and un-accredited laboratory somewhere on the outskirts of Moscow before being sent on to an approved lab. The person in charge of the accredited testing center would then allegedly receive bribes from athletes to make the positive tests disappear. Everything was rigged, it seemed.

I'm not naive. I know that, sadly, doping will probably always be a part of sports, both amateur and professional. So what can we do? We can be vigilant. We can speak out. We can keep encouraging our kids to be honest and above board. We must never be afraid to address and confront these problems, even when it upsets a lot of other people because you're not behaving the way they expect you to. We live in a world where cheaters prosper in a lot of different industries and professions, but that's no excuse to give up the fight.

Do I feel bad for the East German girls? Yes. Do I think that they could be doing more today to keep people from doping? Absolutely.

There are still plenty of lessons to be learned from the story of the 1976 Games. So many athletes wake up today and make the decision to stick a needle in their arm or take a pill or rub some type of ointment on their body in the hopes that it will make them stronger, make them a champion. But they are slowly killing themselves. Society craves champions and over-achievers, but at what cost? Are there still governments out there that are knowingly helping their athletes achieve greatness through doping?

One of the problems with doping is that the punishments for it don't match the extent of the crime. When high-profile athletes cheat, with or without the help of their government, they're not just hurting themselves. They're hurting the sport. They're hurting their country. They're hurting the world. Until the punishments rise to meet these levels of corruption, destruction, and damage, I think this is going to continue to happen over and over again, because nobody is scared of the repercussions. But if these athletes knew that there would be swift, just, and intensely serious punishments? They would think twice before doing anything illegal.

Sports are, at their best, natural, spontaneous, and real. Think about the greatest moments from the Olympics or any other sport, and what it does to your soul when you're watching them. Think of how it elevates your spirit and celebrates the human condition. That's when sports are at their best. But today, when fame and riches await the best in the world, athletes will do whatever it takes to become the best in the world.

As I write this, there are thousands of honest athletes around the world who get cheated by this sort of behavior. They don't get the medals or the sponsorships or the money. They watch the cheaters prosper. My message to all of them is that, no matter what, you should never compromise your integrity or your health. It will never be worth it. Because you'll always know in your heart that you did it the right way, that you properly represented your sport and maybe even your country. That's what really matters. I may not have gotten all the endorsements or fame like a lot of people expected of me, but when I look at those East German athletes today, I feel really bad for them. Their lives were stolen from them. They were cheated. And they'll pay the price for the rest of their lives.

As for me? I don't have one regret. I always swam my heart out and worked as hard as I could. I was blessed with a beautiful son who remains a huge part of my life (along with his love-ly wife). I've never had to regret one second of my career as a swimmer or anything else. I have bonds with the friends I made during my swimming career that will never be broken. Even though, in some cases, we only saw each other two or three times a year, everyone was working toward the same goal: to be your best at the sport you loved. Whenever I see them now, it's like everything happened just a few weeks ago, rather than decades ago.

Nobody can take any of this away from me—especially that one magical moment when three incredible young American women and I did something nobody thought we could do. We accomplished something that even the cheaters couldn't ruin. We beat them fair and square. That's the only way to do it.

Shirley Babashoff's Individual World and American Records

World Records

Date	Event	Time	Place
6/21/1976	800 Freestyle	8:39.63	Long Beach, California
6/20/1975	400 Freestyle	4:14.76	Long Beach, California
8/31/1974	200 Freestyle	2:02.94	Concord, California
8/23/1974	200 Freestyle	2:02.94	Concord, California
8/22/1974	400 Freestyle	4:15.77	Concord, California
8/14/1972	200 Freestyle	2:05.21	Chicago, Illinois

American Records

Date	Event	Time	Place
7/25/1976	800 Freestyle	8:37.59	Montreal, Canada
7/20/1976	400 Freestyle	4:10.46	Montreal, Canada
6/21/1976	800 Freestyle	8:39.63	Long Beach, California
6/20/1976	100 Freestyle	56.95	Long Beach, California
6/19/1976	800 Freestyle	8:46.00	Long Beach, California
6/18/1976	400 Freestyle	4:12.85	Long Beach, California
6/16/1976	200 Freestyle	2:00.69	Long Beach, California

6/16/1976	200 Freestyle	2:02.17	Long Beach, California
8/23/1975	100 Freestyle	57.48	Kansas City, Kansas
8/21/1975	200 Freestyle	2:02.39	Kansas City, Kansas
7/23/1975	200 Freestyle	2:02.50	Cali, Colombia
6/22/1975	100 Freestyle	57.74	Long Beach, California
6/20/1975	400 Freestyle	4:14.76	Long Beach, California
6/19/1975	200 Freestyle	2:02.54	Long Beach, California
8/31/1974	200 Freestyle	2:02.94	Concord, California
8/23/1974	200 Freestyle	2:02.94	Concord, California
8/22/1974	400 Freestyle	4:15.77	Concord, California
9/1/1972	200 Freestyle	2:04.33	Munich, Germany
8/14/1972	200 Freestyle	2:05.21	Chicago, Illinois

An Open Letter to Thomas Bach, President of the International Olympic Committee

⊢———————————————————————⊣

Dear Mr. Bach:

I'm writing you to let you know that I think it is time to give all of the female swimmers from the 1976 Olympics in Montreal their fair due.

I'm not asking that the East Germans be stripped of their medals. Those girls were tools of their country. In my opinion, they never knew what was happening to them and they were out there working as hard as they could. They didn't know they were cheating. In fact, they themselves were cheated by their own government. So I think their medals should be left alone.

But I do think that you could move everyone up in the order. Wherever the East German women won medals in swimming, I think it is fair to say that all of those medals are tainted. So, simply slide everyone up. Give those swimmers the medals they deserve, and let the East Germans keep theirs.

Problem solved.

Think of what you'll be doing for the Olympics. All of the sudden, everyone will be able to move on. Think of the fourth-place finishers that will now have a bronze medal. After forty years, maybe someone will be able to tell her grandchild that yes, she earned an Olympic medal.

There is such an opportunity here for you to do something

that so many people have long wanted. I understand the issues. The East Germans were so far ahead of the science forty years ago that there was no way to really tell what was going on. But just think of what we've learned in the years since the Berlin Wall came down. We know what happened. There is no more mystery.

I worked very hard in the four years leading up to those Olympics and yes, while winning four silvers is certainly something I'm proud of, I also know what would have most likely happened, had it not been for the East German doping. People still talk about how my three teammates and I finally won the gold medal in that memorable relay, and how we changed history. But I don't think it ever should have gotten to that moment, no matter how glorious or triumphant that moment was.

You can make a difference. You can right the wrongs of the past and acknowledge the efforts and accomplishments of so many athletes. Everyone was cheated that year—every athlete, as well as everyone who watched the Games. The world was cheated.

I've been criticized in the past for speaking out, but that never stopped me. In life, I believe you have to call things as you see them. And there would be no more fair gesture that awarding the medals to their proper recipients.

On behalf of the many athletes that this situation affects, I thank you for any consideration that you give this letter. So much time has gone by, and nobody is getting any younger. Hopefully you will agree—now is the time.

Respectfully,
Shirley Babashoff

What the 1976 Olympic Records Would Look Like If They Were Revised

If the 1976 record books were revised today, these would be the final medal standings for the female swimmers at the 1976 Olympics. World records (and Shirley Babashoff's American records) are designated by asterisks.

100 Freestyle
JULY 19, 1976
OLYMPIC FINALISTS:
Kornelia Ender, DDR 55.65*
Petra Priemer, DDR 56.49
Enith Brigitha, HOL 56.65 (Gold)
Kim Peyton, USA 56.81 (Silver)
Shirley Babashoff, USA 56.95 (Bronze)
Claudia Hempel, DDR 56.99
Jill Sterkel, USA 57.06
Jutta Weber, GER 57.26

200 Freestyle

JULY 22, 1976

OLYMPIC FINALISTS:

Kornelia Ender, DDR 1:59.26*

Shirley Babashoff, USA 2:01.22 (Gold)

Enith Brigitha, HOL 2:01.40 (Silver)

Annelies Maas, HOL 2:02.56 (Bronze)

Gail Amundrud, CAN 2:03.32

Jennifer Hooker, USA 2:04.20

Claudia Hempel, DDR 2:04.61

Irina Vlasova, USSR 2:05.63

400 Freestyle

JULY 20, 1976

OLYMPIC FINALISTS:

Petra Thümer, DDR 4:09.89*

Shirley Babashoff, USA 4:10.46 (Gold)*

Shannon Smith, CAN 4:14.60 (Silver)

Rebecca Perrott, NZL 4:14.76 (Bronze)

Kathy Heddy, USA 4:15.50

Brenda Borgh, USA 4:17.43

Annelies Maas, HOL 4:17.44

Sabine Kahle, DDR 14:20.42

800 Freestyle

JULY 25, 1976

WORLD RECORD:

OLYMPIC FINALISTS:

Petra Thümer, DDR 8:37.14*

Shirley Babashoff, USA 8:37.59 (Gold)*

Wendy Weinberg, USA 8:42.60 (Silver)

Rosemary Milgate, AUS 8:47.21 (Bronze)
Nicole Kramer, USA 8:47.33
Shannon Smith, CAN 8:48.15
Regina Jager, DDR 8:50.40
Jenny Turrell, AUS 8:52.88

100 Backstroke
JULY 21, 1976
OLYMPIC FINALISTS:
UIrike Richter, DDR 1:01.83
Birgit Treiber, DDR 1:03.41
Nancy Garapick, CAN 1:03.71 (Gold)
Wendy Hogg, CAN 1:03.93 (Silver)
Cheryl Gibson, CAN 1:05.16 (Bronze)
Nadejda Stavko, USSR 1:05.19
Antje Stille, DDR 1:05.30
Diane Edelijn, HOL 1:05.53

200 Backstroke
JULY 25, 1976
OLYMPIC FINALISTS:
Ulrike Richter, DDR 2:13.43
Birgit Treiber, DDR 2:14.97
Nancy Garapick, CAN 2:15.60 (Gold)
Nadejda Stavko, USSR 2:16.28 (Silver)
Melissa Belote, USA 2:17.27 (Bronze)
Antje Stille, DDR 2:17.55
Klavdia Studennikova, USSR 2:17.74
Wendy Hogg, CAN 2:17.95

100 Breaststroke
JULY 24, 1976
OLYMPIC FINALISTS:
Hannelore Anke, DDR 1:11.16
Lyubov Rusanova, USSR 1:13.04 (Gold)
Marina Koshevaya, USSR 1:13.30 (Silver)
Carola Nitschke, DDR 1:13.33
Gabriele Askamp, GER 1:14.15 (Bronze)
Marina Yurchenia, USSR 1:14.17
Margaret Kelly, GBR 1:14.20
Karla Linke, DDR 1:14.21

200 Breaststroke
JULY 21, 1976
OLYMPIC FINALISTS:
Marina Koshevaya, USSR 2:33.35 (Gold)*
Marina Yurchenia, USSR 2:36.08 (Silver)
Lyubov Rusanova, USSR 2:36.49 (Bronze)
Karla Linke, DDR 2:36.97
Carola Nitschke, DDR 2:38.27
Margaret Kelly, GBR 2:38.37
Deborah Rudd, GBR 2:39.01

100 Butterfly
JULY 22, 1976
OLYMPIC FINALISTS
Kornelia Ender, DDR 1:00.13*
Andrea Pollack, DDR 1:00.98
Wendy Boglioli, USA 1:01.17 (Gold)
Camille Wright, USA 1:01.41 (Silver)

Rosemarie Gabriel, DDR 1:01.56
Wendy Quirk, CAN 1:01.75 (Bronze)
Lelei Fonoimoana, USA 1:01.95
Tamara Shelofastova, USSR 1:02.74

200 Butterfly
JULY 19, 1976
OLYMPIC FINALISTS:
Andrea Pollack, DDR 2:11.41
Ulrike Tauber, DDR 2:12.50
Rosemarie Gabriel, DDR 2:12.86
Karen Thornton, USA 2:12.90 (Gold)
Wendy Quirk, CAN 2:13.68 (Silver)
Cheryl Gibson, CAN 2:13.91 (Bronze)
Tamara Shelofastova, USSR 2:14.26
Natalia Popova, USSR 2:14.50

400 Individual Medley
JULY 24, 1976
OLYMPIC FINALISTS:
Ulrike Tauber, DDR 4:42.77*
Cheryl Gibson, CAN 4:48.10 (Gold)
Becky Smith, CAN 4:50.48 (Silver)
Birgit Treiber, DDR 4:52.40
Sabine Kahle, DDR 4:53.50
Donnalee Wennerstrom, USA 4:55.34 (Bronze)
Joann Baker, CAN 5:00.19
Monique Rodahl, NZL 5:00.21

400 Medley Relay
JULY 18, 1976
OLYMPIC FINALISTS:
DDR: Richter, Anke, Pollack, Ender 4:07.95
USA: Jezek, Siering, Wright, Babashoff 4:14.55 (Gold)
CAN: Hogg, Corsiglia, Sloan, Jardin 4:15.22 (Silver)
USSR: Stavko, Yurchenia, Shelofastova, Tsareva 4:16.05
      (Bronze)
HOL: Edelijn, Mazereeuw, Damen, Brigitha 4:19.93
GBR: Beasley, Kelly, Jenner, Hill 4:23.25
JPN: Nishigawa, Haruoka, Hatsuda, Yamazaki 4:23.47
AUS: de Vries, Hudson, Hanel, Tate 4:25.91

400 Freestyle Relay
JULY 25, 1976
OLYMPIC FINALISTS:
USA: Peyton, Boglioli, Sterkel, Babashoff 3:44.82 (Gold)*
DDR: Ender, Priemer, Pollack, Hempel 3:45.50
CAN: Amundrud, Clark, Smith, Jardin 3:48.81 (Silver)
HOL: Ran, Faber, Maas, Brigitha 3:51.67 (Bronze)
USSR: Kobzova, Vlasova, Kliuchnikova, Tsareva 3:52.69
FRA: Berger, Le Noach, Carpentier, Schertz 3:56.73
SWE: Martensson, Persson, Olsson, Hansson 3:57.25
GER: Weber, Platten, Nissen, Jasch 3:58.33

Notes from Coaches
Jim Montrella and
Mark Schubert

├───┤

Jim Montrella
1976 Olympic Team Coach

Thanks to Shirley, a lot of people became aware that something really wrong was taking place with the East German team at the '76 Games. But honestly, for me it was nothing new. Back in 1970, I had been in Barcelona for the European Swimming Championships and even then we knew something strange was going on. You could see it in the swimmers. They were a lot better than they had been in the last year or two, and nobody simply gets that much better that fast without drugs. It just doesn't happen. But we didn't know enough then to prove anything, so all we could do was observe and prepare our own teams to swim extra hard. That was the mentality back then: Just work harder.

But then the '72 Games in Munich came and the East Germans didn't do very well. Maybe they missed taking their drugs or something, I remember thinking. Maybe their timing was off and they simply hadn't figured out yet what it took to maximize whatever it was that they were doing. So by the time the '76 Games rolled around, for six years or so I had been thinking about that team, watching them develop over the years and getting frustrated that there was nothing anyone could do about it. We just knew we had our work cut out for us whenever we went up against the East Germans.

I had two roles on the '76 team: I was an assistant coach and also an assistant manager. I never got involved with the media—that was Jack Nelson's job, our head coach. But I did play a big part in getting the relay team together for that final race, and it's something I'll always be very proud of. In the days leading up to the relay, Shirley was so busy with all of her other competitions, so I took the other three girls and began working with them off-site at a pool away from the Olympic Village. Our girls, Wendy, Kim, and Jill, knew that Shirley was going to be the anchor, and they were sworn to secrecy. We knew that if we were going to win, we couldn't let anything get out beforehand. Our strategy had to remain private.

Shirley just seemed like the perfect anchor. She was so strong and so determined, and we felt that if the teams only learned that on the day of the race, then they would know they were up against something pretty hard to beat. Shirley was such an impact swimmer—we all felt that if we basically stayed near, even through the first three swimmers, then Shirley would bring it home.

Starting off with Kim against Kornelia also made sense to us. Kim was just an amazing swimmer and very tough-minded. I told her, "Look, your job is to simply stay as close to her as you can. Don't give her more than a body length, stay close to the lane line, and we should be okay. That's all you need to do." Next would be Wendy. Wendy was also very special. Really more of an adult than most of the other kids. She was very sharp and tough and we knew that she would pick up right where Kim left off and stay as close as she needed to. Wendy was one of our captains and a great leader. Jill was the youngest of them, just fifteen, and we thought she'd be the right spark plug in the third position before handing it over to Shirley.

I watched that race from the top row of the United States section in the bleachers, and I was standing the entire time. The whole time, watching that race unfold before me, I don't think I had ever been as excited. It began just as we thought. Kim stayed close to Ender. Wendy did the same thing, completely did her job, and then you had Jill, who swam her heart out as the others did and after the first length, took that dramatic lead. When she pulled ahead, we all went crazy because we knew who was waiting for her at the other end. Shirley. And there was no way Shirley was going to give up that lead.

Watching them hug each other and jump up and down like little kids at the end of that race was one of the most satisfying experiences I ever had as a coach. They all did exactly what they needed to do and they beat a team that everyone knew was cheating. That is, everyone who was paying attention.

Shirley was the one the media always wanted to get to, and so she became like a representative for the entire team. And she did what a lot of young people do when they get threatened. She fought back. I think about it today and I still get angry. But I'm also reminded that I think we really let those kids down in a certain way. We never gave them the tools about how to deal with the media. All of the issues with the drugs were way beyond us. It was too new, there were too many uncertainties, and it was very political, obviously. So there was nothing we could do about that. Had we trained them, especially Shirley, in how to deal with the media, maybe afterwards she would've had some contracts or endorsements the way other athletes did. It wouldn't change the results of the Olympics obviously, but the perception of her would've been different. I don't blame her for speaking out the way she did. She was always honest and always called it like she saw it. But we could've done a much better job of teaching that team not only how to swim faster but also how to deal with life. We failed them.

That said, there is no doubt in my mind that every single female swimmer who finished behind an East German should be given the next highest medal. No question at all. Every one of those swimmers on the East German team was drugged. It was a state-supported system, and there's no way they would've left any of those athletes alone. They were all part of it. I feel terrible for those East German girls. But that's how it happened. We know that now. If the IOC doesn't do anything about it, then I think the United States Olympic Committee should do something. All of those athletes, from our country and others, were all cheated by the East Germans. And I think it's a disgrace that forty years have gone by and nothing's really been done about it.

Mark Schubert
Shirley's Personal Coach, 1972–1976

My perception about Shirley is a little different than most, I think, because I had such a unique perspective as her coach. I will always think of her from my experiences watching her practice and then from my experience with her at the Olympic Trials in 1976. I think her accomplishments there are still some of the greatest sports performances in U.S. history. To win five events like she did was just stunning. Remarkable. Long Beach was a special competition for her. She was a national champion numerous times and an Olympic medalist, of course, and was very famous as probably the world's foremost swimmer going into that meet. What she has done, in my view, has never been equaled. To win every freestyle event and the individual medley . . . it really was just an incredible feat.

And, of course, I think what happened in Montreal was a travesty. I think she should be awarded those gold medals in the events in which she placed second, and I think all kids who were cheated by the East Germans in all of those competitions should be properly awarded.

I understand the IOC's position on that, because a lot of the cheating can't be proven, but I think the cheating that *was* proven should be acknowledged officially and the medals presented to the people who deserve them. We certainly know enough today about what was going on to make the proper adjustments.

Of all the people I've worked with, nobody worked harder than Shirley. She competed against the men more than any other female that I coached and she just took on anybody in practice. It didn't matter. She was so competitive. She came in every day with her work boots on to do whatever I asked her to do without question. It was really a joy to work with such a sincere and marvelous young lady.

I'll also never forget that day she quit in '76 before the Trials. I was certainly nervous because I understood the pressure that she was under, but I hoped that it was just a teenage moment. After we talked at length, I was very relieved to know that she did want to continue and would follow through. I think the result of Long Beach Trials was pretty telling in itself—a testament to her commitment and dedication.

She was always very impressive with her maturity and focus in swimming, but I saw a definite difference over the years in that she became a young woman emotionally and even more mature as she endured what she did. She became the scapegoat in 1976, but today, the world has changed and both the world and the swimming community have tremendous respect for Shirley. She is a remarkable woman. A leader. Always has been. Always will be.

About the Authors

Shirley Babashoff was the most successful female U.S. Olympian prior to the 1990s, with a total of eight Olympic medals. Although she never won an individual Olympic gold medal, she is recognized as one of the greatest freestyle swimmers of all time. Babashoff set eleven world records (six in individual events and an additional five in relay events) and also set thirty-nine U.S. records (seventeen individual and twenty-two relay). At one point, she held the U.S. freestyle record at every distance from 100-meter to 800-meter.

Apart from her record-breaking ability, Babashoff had a fine competitive record in major championships, winning—including relays—twenty-seven AAU titles, in addition to taking the 200-meter and 400-meter individual gold medals at the 1975 World Championships. Her greatest performance ever came at the 1976 Olympic Trials, where she won every freestyle event and the 400-meter individual medley. She set three U.S. records in the heats and three more in the finals, and broke the world record in the 800-meter freestyle. This ranks among the greatest swimming feats of all time.

Babashoff was infamously vilified by many in the media in 1976 because she complained that the East German swimmers who had defeated her, notably Kornelia Ender, were obviously using performance-enhancing drugs (PEDs). After the fall of the Berlin Wall in 1990, documents from the East German secret police, the Stasi, were found that confirmed all of

Babashoff's suspicions.

On April 30, 2005, Babashoff received the Olympic Order, the highest award of the Olympic Movement, during the Inaugural Olympic Assembly Luncheon. International Olympic Committee members Bob Ctvrtlik, Anita DeFrantz, and Jim Easton presented the award. The IOC established the Olympic Order in 1974 to honor individuals who have illustrated the Olympic ideals through their actions, achieved remarkable merit in the sporting world, or rendered outstanding services to the Olympic cause, either through their own personal achievements or their contributions to the development of sport.

Chris Epting is the author/photographer of twenty-five travel and history books, including *James Dean Died Here*, *Roadside Baseball*, *Marilyn Monroe Dyed Here*, *The Birthplace Book* (Stackpole Books), and many others. He has also co-written memoirs with Def Leppard guitarist Phil Collen and legendary Rock and Roll Hall of Famer John Oates. Epting is an award-winning travel writer and music journalist and has contributed articles for such publications as the *Los Angeles Times*, *Westways*, and *Travel + Leisure*. Originally from New York, Epting now lives in Huntington Beach, California, with his wife and two children.

Acknowledgments

Shirley Babashoff

There are many people that I need to acknowledge and thank, and if I forget anyone, I'm deeply sorry. To my son, Adam, and his lovely wife, Laura, I love you very much. To all of my coaches over the years and all of my teammates, I owe you more than I can ever repay. To my good friends Tony and Donna, and everyone I work with at the post office, thank you for everything. To Chris Epting and his wonderful family, especially his mom, Sugar, without whom I would never have met Chris. Thank you for making me feel like part of your family. To my dog, Duke, for always being there for me. To Mike Unger and everyone at Team USA Swimming, thank you for everything. Same to Brent Rutemiller and his amazing staff at *Swimming World Magazine*. Without them, I don't think the issues of the 1976 Games would even be on the table. Bruce Wigo, I appreciate all you do on behalf of swimmers at the International Swimming Hall of Fame. Great job! Thank you to Donna de Varona for her kind words in this book and thanks as well to John Naber, Mark Spitz, and Sammy Lee. To Karen Crause, for her wonderful journalistic skills. To Jeffrey Goldman, Kate Murray, and Amy Inouye at Santa Monica Press, thank you so much for all the hard work in helping to put this book together. And thank you to all of the fans over the years for their support and belief in me. I'm deeply grateful for you.

Chris Epting

Shirley, thank you for being the woman you are. It is a privilege to know you as a friend, and it was an honor to work on this with you. Thanks to my family, as always, for their reliable support through projects like this. A big thank you to Robyn Plaster for her editorial assistance, and my friend Jeffrey Goldman at Santa Monica Press for his faith and support in this project. Thanks as well to Kate Murray and Amy Inouye at Santa Monica Press. For my part in this book, I dedicate it to my dear friend Rich Bertolucci, who passed away while Shirley and I were writing it. Rich always loved Shirley's story and could not wait for this book to be completed, and my one wish is that he could have seen it.

Index

AAU Championships, **x**, 96, 105, 112, 189
ABC, 9–10, 62, 91, 139, 141, 179
ABC's Wide World of Sports, 91
Adidas, 74, 180
Albert II, Prince of Monaco, 106
Ali, Muhammad, 103
American record, 96, 106, 109, 119–121, 178, 189, 224, 245–246
Amundrud, Gail, 250, 254
androstenedione, 211
Andy Griffith Show, The, 98
Anke, Hannelore, 252, 254
Aquatic World, 104
Arena, **xxvii–xxviii**, 179–183, 188
Arena's Elite Team, **xxvii**, 180
Armstrong, Lance, 225
Askamp, Gabriele, 252
Associated Press, 110, 197
Atwood, Susie, **viii**
Australian Swimming Championships, 169

Babashoff, Adam, **xxix**, 194, 199, 204–206, 243
Babashoff, Bill, **ii**, 17–20, 30, 33
Babashoff, Debbie, **xi**, 27, 37, 175, 192
Babashoff, Jack, **ii**, 19–27, 30, 33, 38–41, 48, 140–141, 185, 188, 201, 236–237
Babashoff, Jack, Jr., **ii**, 17, 19, 20, 23, 25, 30, 33, 123, 127, 172

Babashoff, Vera, **ii**, 17, 19, 20–34, 37–41, 44–45, 48, 55, 58, 77–79, 82, 85–86, 117, 140, 155, 173–175, 184–185, 188, 199, 200–201, 237
Bach, Thomas, 247
Baker, Joann, 253
Barkman, Jane, **vii**, 67, 68
Bayless, Skip, **xvi**, 123–125
Beasley, Joy, 254
Behnisch, Gunther, 64
Belmont Plaza Pool, **v**, 107, 118
Belmont Shore, 80
Belote, Melissa, **ix**, 91, 251
Berger, Guylaine, 254
Berger, Paul, 77
Berlin Wall, 200, 213, 231, 248
Biondi, Matt, 196
Black September, 75
blood tests, 93, 102
Boglioli, Wendy, **xxii–xxiv**, 119, 147–148, 154, 158–163, 195, 234, 252, 254, 256–257
Borgh, Brenda, 250
Boston Globe, 214
Brigitha, Enith, 52, 144, 146, 249–250, 254
Brown, Brian, 233–234
Brundage, Avery, 64
Bryant, Bear, 59
Buena Park Splashers, **v**, 23, 107

Calhoun, Kathy, **v**
Calligaris, Novella, **xxvii**, 180
Canseco, José, 212
Carpentier, Caroline, 254

Cerritos College, 22
Charlie's Angels, 179
Chavoor, Sherm, 59
Checkpoint Charlie, 53
Clark, Barbara, 254
Colella, Rick, 165
Concord Community Park, 98
Corsiglia, Robin, 254
Counsilman, James "Doc," 70
Crabbe, Buster, 191
Crandal Pool, 126
Crouse, Karen, 216, 240–241
Crystal Palace, 85
Ctvrtlik, Bob, 219
Cuyahoga Falls High School, 80

Damen, José, 254
Darr, Ralph "Flip," **xii**, 34, 36,
    43–48, 51, 55–59, 62, 66–70,
    80–81, 83, 86, 95, 99, 107–108,
    110, 236
Dassler, Horst, 180
de Varona, Donna, **xix**, 9, 96, 139,
    155, 195–196, 221
de Vries, Michelle, 254
DeFrantz, Anita, 219
Deutsche Welle magazine, 230
Dibiasi, Klaus, **xxvii**, 180
Disneyland, **ix**, 53, 74, 80, 85, 174,
    176, 191
DNA test, 65, 134
doping. *See* performance-
    enhancing drugs (PEDs)
Douglas, Kirk, 85
drug test, 66, 99
drug trafficking, 225
Duke, Sherry, 30
Dwight's (concession stand), 117

East Los Angeles College, 105
Easton, Jim, 219
Edelijn, Diane, 251, 254
Eife, Andrea, 68

Elm, Frank, 126, 160
Ender, Kornelia, **xx**, **xxix**, 68–69,
    91–92, 98, 100, 109–110,
    136, 139, 144, 146, 154, 161,
    174, 203, 205–206, 226, 234,
    249–250, 252, 254, 256–257
Erving, Julius, 103
European Swimming
    Championships, 255
Evans, Janet, 196
Ewald, Manfred, 213

Faber, Linda, 254
Fawcett, Farrah, 179
FINA, 9–10, 86–87, 91, 231–232
FINA World Aquatics
    Championships, **xii–xiii**, 9,
    86–92, 95, 104–108, 110, 111,
    136, 145–146, 148, 150, 189,
    192, 197, 232
First Annual World Invitational
    Swim Meet, 85
Fonoimoana, Lelei, 253
Ford, Gerald, **xvii**, 113, 128–129,
    130
Fountain Valley High School, 55,
    77–78, 84, 103
Friendship Games, 191
Furniss, Steve, **xxvii**, 100, 180

Gabriel, Rosemarie, 253
Garapick, Nancy, 251
Garvey, Steve, 103
Geipel, Ines, 230
Gergen, Joe, 170–172
German Sports Federation, 201
Geweniger, Ute, 203, 226
Giambi, Jason, 212
Gibson, Cheryl, 251, 253
Gillette Cavalcade of Champions,
    103
Golden Goggle Awards, **xxxi**, 221
Golden Goggle Female Athlete of
    the Year Award, 221

Golden West College, **xiii**, 34, 56, 80, 103, 109, 112, 185
González, Juan, 212
Goodell, Brian, **xxv**, 81, 113, 127, 172
Gould, Shane, **ix**, 57–58, 63, 65, 67, 69–70, 85, 88–89, 92, 116
Gowdy, Curt, 221
Graddy, Sam, 197
Grummt, Steffen, 206
Guinness Book of World Records, The, 50
Guthrie, Janet, 179

Hall, Gary, **xxvii**, 48–49, 180
Hamill, Kelly, **x**, **xiii**, 102, 112
hand paddles, 34, 56
Hanel, Linda, 254
Hansson, Ida, 254
Harshbarger, Jo, 62–63, 73
Haruoka, Toshiko, 254
Hatsuda, Yasue, 254
Heddy, Kathy, 89, 97, 100, 107–111, 119, 126, 135, 223, 250
Heidenreich, Jerry, 72
Hempel, Claudia, 156, 249–250, 254
Hencken, John, 100
Hermstad, Tom "Herm," 103, 186
Hill, Debbie, 254
Hoeppner, Manfred, 213
Hogg, Wendy, 251, 254
Homecoming Queen, **xiii**, 112
Hooker, Jennifer, 250
Hope, Bob, 103
Horner, Silke, 226
Hübner, Andrea, 91
Hudson, Judith, 254
Huntington Beach Aquatic Club, 48, 55, 57
Huntington Beach Post Office, 199, 203, 215–216
Hybl, Bill, 208

Indiana University, 70, 206
International Invitational, 96
International Olympic Committee (IOC), 10, 64, 177, 203, 208, 211, 213–214, 217, 219, 220, 224–226, 231, 240, 247, 258–259
International Swimming Hall of Fame, 43, 115, 188

Jager, Regina, 251
James E. Sullivan Award, 43, 71, 172
Japanese National Championships, 112
Jardin, Anne, 254
Jasch, Beate, 254
Jaws, 107
Jenapharm, 220
Jenner, Bruce, 130–131, 221
Jenner, Sue, 254
Jezek, Linda, 143, 208, 254
Johnson, Ben, 197–198
Juiced, 212

Kahle, Sabine, 250, 253
Kardashians, 221
Kelly, Grace, 106
Kelly, Margaret, 252, 254
Kemp, Jennifer, **vii**, 67, 68
King, Billie Jean, 103
King, Maxine "Micki," **xxvii**, 180
Kipke, Lothar, 232
Kliuchnikova, Marina, 254
Knape, Ulrika, **xxvii**, 180
Kobzova, Lyubov, 254
Koshevaya, Marina, 252
Kramer, Nicole, 151, 251
Krause, Barbara, **xix**, 145, 160, 203, 226
Kreischa doping laboratory, 201
Kremlin, 52
Krumpholz, Kurt, 86

Lacour, Jean-Pierre, 92
LaMont, Don, **iii**, **v**, 30
Last Gold, The, 233–234
Le Noach, Sylvie, 254
Lee, Sammie, 193
Lee, Valerie, **x**
Lewis, Carl, 197–198
Lightfoot, Gordon, 140
Linke, Karla, 252
Long Beach Press-Telegram, 121
Lord, Craig, 233
Los Angeles Invitational, 97
Los Angeles Times, **xv–xvi**, 78, 123, 174, 201, 203
Louganis, Greg, 80

Maas, Annelies, 250, 254
Major League Baseball, 212
Mandela, Nelson, 231
Marguerite Aquatic Center, 80
Marshall, Ann, 70, 100
Martensson, Pia, 254
Matthes, Roland, 100, 110
May, Scott, **xvi**, 127
Mazereeuw, Wijda, 254
McGaugh Elementary School, 186
McGwire, Mark, 211–212
Meyer, Debbie, 43
Milgate, Rosemary, 251
Miracle on Ice, 187, 205
Mission Viejo High School, 80–81, 103, 113, 173
Mission Viejo Invitational, 111
Mission Viejo Reporter, 121
Mohring, Anke, 226
Montrella, Jim, 255–258
Mount San Antonio Senior Meet, 96
Mulroney, Brian, 198
Munich massacre, 72–75, 133

Naber, John, **xxxi**, 98, 100, 127, 172

Nadadores, 80, 112, 189
Natatorium, 105, 155
National Football League, 211
NCAA, 70
negative split, 57, 66–67
Neilson, Sandy, **v**, **vii–viii**, 30, 65, 67–68
Nelson, Jack, 99, 124–126, 160, 174, 222–225, 234–236, 256
New Times Broward-Palm Beach, 235
New York Times, 202, 207, 213, 216, 234, 240
Newsday, 170
Newsweek, 240
Nicklaus, Jack, 103
Nishigawa, Yoshimi, 254
Nissen, Regina, 254
Nitschke, Carola, 252
Nixon, Richard, **viii**, 46, 79
Norwalk Brethren School, 23
Norwalk High School, 22
Nyad, Diana, 235–236

Olsson, Diana, 254
Olympia Schwimmhalle, 65
Olympiastadion, 64
Olympic Games (1936), 64
Olympic Games (1948), 193
Olympic Games (1968), 43, 70
Olympic Games (1972), **vii–viii**, **ix**, 44, 53, 55, 58–79, 85–86, 91, 99, 104, 110, 114, 124–125, 144, 180, 189, 214, 255
Olympic Games (1976), **xv–xxv**, 77, 84, 86, 96, 101, 104, 109–110, 113–114, 123, 128–178, 187, 189, 191, 195, 205, 208, 212–217, 219, 221, 224, 233, 239, 240, 247–249, 255, 258
Olympic Games (1979), 186–188
Olympic Games (1980), 176
Olympic Games (1984), 115, 191

Olympic Games (1988), 193,
196–197
Olympic Games (1992), 204–205
Olympic Games (2008), 221
*Olympic Games: A Social Science
Perspective, The*, 214
Olympic Hall of Fame, 195
Olympic Order, 219
Olympic Stadium, 135
Olympic Trials, **vi**, **xv**, 44, 57–58,
69, 71, 113, 116–124, 158, 189,
197, 213, 239, 258–259
Olympic Village, 54, 61–62, 72–74,
133, 135, 137–140, 145–148,
160, 162, 256
opening ceremonies, 63–64, 108,
142
Oprah Winfrey Show, The, 225
Otto, Kristin, **xxx**, 196, 226
Owens, Jesse, 128

Palestine Liberation Organization,
75
Palm Beach Post, 216
Palmeiro, Rafael, 212
Pan American Games, 34, 70, 111
People Are Talking, 235
performance-enhancing drugs
(PEDs), **xix–xx**, **xxx**, 9–10, 90,
93, 159, 191, 198, 201–217,
220–234, 240–242, 248,
257–258
Perrott, Rebecca, 250
Persson, Ylva, 254
Peyton, Kim, **xxi–xxiv**, 98,
100, 119–120, 147–148, 154,
158–163, 165, 195, 222, 234,
249, 254, 256–257
Phelps, Michael, **xxxi**, 71
Phillips 66 (swim team), 34, 85
Platten, Marion, 254
Pollack, Andrea, **xx**, 154–155,
252–254

Popova, Natalia, 253
Powers, John, 214
Priemer, Petra, 144, 154, 161, 249,
254
Puma, 74, 163

Quirk, Wendy, 253

Ran, Ineke, 254
Red Cross, 22, 186
Reed, Loretta, 32–34
Reed, Pam, **v**, 32–33
retirement, **xxvi**, 177
Richter, Ulrike, **xx**, 91, 203, 251,
254
Riley, John, 29–30
Rodahl, Monique, 253
Rodríguez, Iván, 212
Rogge, Jacques, 208
Roosevelt, Franklin D., 128
Rothhammer, Keena, **viii**, 70
Rudd, Deborah, 252
Runyon, Marvin, 204
Rusanova, Lyubov, 252
Rutemiller, Brent, 222–223, 233

Santa Clara Invitational, 97
Schertz, Chantal, 254
Schneider, Petra, 203, 226
Schoenfield, Dana, **viii**
Schollander, Don, **xiv**, **xxvii**, 92
Schubert, Mark, **xiv–xv**, **xxv**,
80–83, 86, 94–97, 102–105,
112, 114, 117–120, 123–126,
137–138, 143–145, 157, 177–
178, 193, 196, 213, 224–225,
236, 239–240, 255, 258–259
Shelofastova, Tamara, 253–254
Shirley Babashoff Day, 78
Shorter, Frank, **xvi**, 127
Siering, Lauri, 143, 208, 254
Simpson, O. J., 140–141
Sirch, Cornelia, 226

skinsuit, 91, 95–96, 100, 102, 105, 144
Sloan, Tara, 254
Smith, Becky, 253–254
Smith, Jaclyn, 179
Smith, Shannon, 151, 250–251
Sosa, Sammy, 211–212
Sound of Music, The, 74
Southern California Invitational, 96, 105
Speedo, 179
Spitz, Mark, **xxvii**, 7–8, 10, 61, 63, 70–75, 92, 96, 121, 130, 180–181
Sports Illustrated, **xvi**, **xxix**, 27, 95, 115, 127, 205–206, 217
St. Basil's Cathedral, 52
"Star-Spangled Banner, The," **xxiii**, 157
Starbuck, JoJo, 179
Stasi, 202
State University of New York at Plattsburgh, **xvii**, 126–127
Stavko, Nadejda, 251, 254
Sterkel, Jill, **xxii–xxiv**, 13–16, 30, 119, 121, 147–148, 154–155, 158–165, 195, 234, 249, 254–257
steroids. *See* performance-enhancing drugs (PEDs)
Stille, Antje, 251
Studennikova, Klavdia, 251
Superstars, The, 179, 185
"Surly Shirley," **xvi**, 14, 124–125, 137, 147, 171, 177, 214, 217
Swimming World, **xv**, **xxvi**, **xxx**, 92–93, 101, 104, 155–156, 172, 189, 208–209, 216, 220, 222, 225–226, 231, 233
Swimming World European Swimmer of the Year award, 226, 231

Swimming World Female American Swimmer of the Year award, 104, 189
Swimming World Male World Swimmer of the Year award, 172
Swimming World World Swimmer of the Year award, 226, 231
SwimVortex.com, 231, 233

Taillibert, Roger, 135
Tasmajdan Sports Centre, 87
Tate, Jenny, 254
Tauber, Ulrike, 109, 226, 253
Thornton, Karen, 253
Thümer, Petra, **xix**, 121, 145, 151, 250
Time, 173
Title IX, 84
Tolan, Eddie, 128
Torres, Dara, 80
Tour de France, 225
Tournament of Roses Parade, 176
Treiber, Birgit, **xx**, 251, 253
Tsareva, Larisa, 254
Turrell, Jenny, 150–151, 251
20/20, 203

U.S. Swimming National Championships, **vi**, 35–36, 43–48, 80, 83, 85–86, 97–101, 106–107
Unger, Mike, 233
Unidad Deportiva Panamericana, 108
United States Anti-Doping Agency, 9, 217, 225
United States Bicentennial, 113
United States Olympic Committee, 208, 258
United States Postal Service, 204, 225
University of California, Los Angeles, 175, 178

UPI, 177
U.S.A. Sportswoman of the Year,
    189
USA Today, 213

vaccine, 93, 101, 167, 222
Vassallo, Jesse, 114–115
Velodrome, 135
Village News, 74
Vlasova, Irina, 250, 254
Vogel, Renate, 91, 214–215

Weber, Jutta, 249, 254
Weinberg, Wendy, 151, 250
Wennerstrom, Donnalee, 253
West Point Military Academy,
    123–126, 138, 159, 224
Western Olympic Development
    Meet, 106
Wheeler, Cozette, **v**, 30
Whitaker, Susie, 35
Wilkie, David, **xxvii**, 180
William Peak Park, 107
Windeatt, Graham, 169–170
Wizard of Oz, The, 53
World Anti-Doping Agency, 9, 240
World Masters Championships,
    206
world record, 14, 34, 49, 58–59,
    67–71, 88, 91–92, 95, 98,
    100, 106–109, 118, 120–122,
    126, 143–146, 151, 154, 156,
    172–178, 180, 189, 197–198,
    215, 224, 232, 245
World Swimming Championship
    Trials, 106
Wright, Camille, 111, 135, 143,
    208, 252, 254
Wylie, Jennifer, 62, 74

Yamazaki, Kyoko, 254
Yurchenia, Marina, 252, 254

Photo Credits

All uncredited photos are from the author's personal collection.

Friedrich Gahlbeck, German Federal Archives: xix (bottom)

Wolfgang Kluge, German Federal Archives: xx (top)

Bjain Berg, *Swimming World*: xx (bottom)

Chris Epting: xxxi (all)

Keleigh Layton: xxxii